ESSENTIAL

Modernityscotland

Revision Notes for
Higher Modern Studies

2011

Essential Modernityscotland

Published by Modernity Publishing
Copyright 2011 John McTaggart
www.modernityscotland.co.uk

EISBN 978-0-9555750-4-4

CONTENTS

INTRODUCTION

Let's be honest. Exams are stressful times. You're not reading this book for fun. You've got an exam in Higher Modern Studies coming up and you want to get the best possible marks you can.

Well, the first thing you need to do is calm down! You probably know a great deal already. If this book provides some kind of reassurance that you are on the right track, that's fine. If it fills in some blanks in your knowledge, that's fine too.

But, let's be clear. These are revision notes. They are chunks of advice and knowledge. Hopefully ones you can remember easily and use in your essays. But, they are no substitute for discussion with your teacher in class.

The good news is that this book won't bamboozle you with loads of complicated advice. Higher Modern Studies, like all Highers, is not, as they say, aeronautic engineering. Sensible, do-able preparations will get you where you want to be.

TECHNIQUE

Answering Paper One Questions

You have to answer four questions in 90 minutes.

One must be from a UK Political Issues Study Theme. One must be from UK Social Issues Wealth and Health Inequalities (there only is one Study Theme here). One must be from an International Issues Study Theme. The last one must be from either a Political Issues in the UK or an International Issues Study Theme.

All questions are worth 15 marks.

How long should I spend on each essay?

You need to be disciplined with your time. Take no longer than 22 minutes for each essay.

This includes reading the question, thinking about your answer, planning it, writing it and having a wee read over it. Do not spend longer than this, especially with the first questions. You will speed up and believe it or not shave a minute or two off the later questions, giving you time to go back.

Four solid questions are much better than three crackers and one disaster. Don't throw away your A pass by getting 1/15 on the last question through bad time management. Take a sports watch into the exam. Give yourself exactly 22 minutes for each question, then move on.

Can I predict the questions?

Well, you can try! You may well be able to predict the topic the question will ask about. But, you are unlikely to be able to predict the exact wording of the question. And, it's the exact wording that counts.

One of the big mistakes many students make is to have a

prepared answer in their head. You can understand why many students do this. You only have 22 minutes per question. Time is at a premium. But, if you don't answer the question, you do not get the best possible marks. So, look at the key phrases in the question. For example,

> *"Assess the impact of the Additional Member System on representation within the Scottish Parliament".*

Don't just write down all you know about the Additional Member System. Highlight key words such as "impact" and "representation". This is what you need to write about.

Make a plan. Brainstorm and perhaps do a spider diagram with all your key points and examples. Five minutes spent on doing this will be much more productive than 22 minutes writing down a memorised answer which does not answer the question.

Yes, but some questions always come up, don't they?

Do not be fooled into believing that certain questions are "bankers". You really need to know the whole Study Theme you have been taught.

How many points do I need to make to get 15/15?

3 or 4 good, well- balanced points, with examples if possible.

What does a good point look like?

How about this one, to the above question on the impact of the Additional Member System on representation within the Scottish Parliament....

> *"The Additional Member System has had a massive impact on representation in the Scottish Parliament. 56 MSPs are elected on the party list system. This has enabled the SNP, which does much better than Labour in the party list vote, to become the Government of Scotland. If we had a First Past the Post System, it is unlikely we would have had an SNP Government in the Scottish Parliament".*

Can you see why this is a good point?

It answers the question, directly. It gives a good, up to date example. It doesn't have lots of statistics. But it contains excellent knowledge and understanding of the impact the Additional Member System has had on representation.

How do I write a balanced answer?

A balanced answer is very important. But balance does not mean that every point you make has to be counter-balanced by an opposite point.

For example, in the above question, there is no doubt that the Additional Member System has had an impact on representation in the Scottish Parliament. It would be plain daft, almost impossible in fact, to write that it hasn't.

So, most of your points may be about the big impact the Additional Member System has had. But other things have had an impact on representation in the Scottish Parliament as well. For example, there aren't any minority ethnic MSPs in the Scottish Parliament (January 2011). There's not a lot the Additional Member System can do if ethnic minorities do not participate in politics, or if parties do not select minority ethnic candidates.

In all the questions, across all the Study Themes, there are alternative viewpoints and arguments.

It's not a matter of having to write 3 points for and 3 points against. That's artificial.

So long as you write balanced comments, which, depending on the question, show that you have evaluated different points of view, you will write a good essay.

Do I need a conclusion at the end of my essay?

There is no point wasting time by repeating at the end what you have already written.

Balanced viewpoints, supported with examples, are what is required. Phrases like "on the other hand" or "alternatively, others might argue that…." are very good. These show that you are providing an alternative explanation.

Should I bother with past papers then if it all comes down to answering the question on the day?

Absolutely! Answering past papers is fantastic preparation. But, only if you do two things.

First, try to answer the question in exam like conditions. No books in front of you, 22 minutes per question. By all means swot up by reading over the issues beforehand. But, if you can, time yourself and try and do the essay the way you'll have to in the exam.

Anyone can write brilliant essays if you've all night to do it. Anyone can copy and paste a brilliant essay. But, writing a good, well balanced essay with examples, in 22 minutes isn't easy. Practice certainly helps.

Second, get your timed essay marked! Your teacher will be impressed (or should be) if you have been practicing essay writing. So, ask to get it marked. And not just with a grade on it. Ask about your strengths and weaknesses. If it's a fail, ask what you need to do to get a C pass. If it's a C, ask what you need to do to get more marks the next time. If you don't know where you're going wrong, you can't improve.

Ask about your technique. Does your essay answer the question? Does it have balanced comments? Does it have accurate, up to date examples?

So, sum up for me what I need to do.

Get past paper questions. These are free, on the Modern Studies pages of the SQA website.

Practice essays in an exam like environment.

Get feedback from your teacher.

Take a sports watch and highlighter pen into the exam.

Allocate 22 minutes for each question.

Highlight key words in the question.

Make a plan with balanced comments and examples.

Model Answer Paper One

Remember, it is important to look at the actual question, then plan, and then write your answer. Too many students write pre-prepared answers which do not answer the question set.

The most important thing is to master the *technique* of answering questions properly.

This example is for Study Theme 2 Social Issues in the UK, Wealth and Health Inequalities.

Q: To what extent is there a link between income and health?

A: *There is a very strong link between income and health. Life expectancy in a rich area like Kensington is about twenty years more than life expectancy in the east end of Glasgow. The parts of Scotland with the highest rates of drug and alcohol abuse are the poorest areas, for example, Dundee, Inverclyde and West Dunbartonshire. Suicide rates are highest in these areas too. If a person has a low income then they are more likely to have poor health for a whole number of reasons.*

Firstly, poorer people are more likely to consume "junk food". They have less income and tend to choose meals which fill themselves and their children up, rather than have the highest nutritional value. There is a strong connection between poverty and low educational attainment. It may be that poorer people eat the wrong foods and/or drink too much because of a lack of education.

On the other hand, these days schools spend a lot of time educating young people about diet and bad lifestyle choices. So, there has to be a better reason to explain the link between income and health.

Health is not just physical health, it is mental health too. People on lower incomes have lower self esteem and fewer ambitions in life. They are more likely to live for the day, than plan for the long term. So, while it is a lifestyle choice they make, to eat the wrong foods and drink to excess, we need to tackle poverty before we are going to really make a difference in health inequalities. In areas like Sighthill in Edinburgh, there aren't a lot of affordable sporting facilities, and young people will also face peer group pressure to drink unhealthily.

We can contrast this with the higher income groups, sometimes referred to as the "worried well". They do act on government campaigns and understand, from an early age, the importance of diet and exercise. People who live in areas like Morningside in Edinburgh are more likely to consult health professionals. They also know how to get the best out of the system as they are professionals themselves. It's no surprise their health is better than those on low incomes.

Another point to make is that it's not just poorer people who make bad lifestyle choices. Many middle class people eat and drink too much too. Alcohol abuse and obesity affect all Scots, regardless of their social class. This is where Dr Harry Burns' studies are important. His biology of poverty report tells us that while the middle classes can lead unhealthy lifestyles, it doesn't impact on them the way it does with poorer people. That's because their bodies' immune systems haven't been damaged from an early age by stress. Burns concludes that we need to look at both unhealthy lifestyles but also intervene earlier in children's lives to improve their well being from the start.

Modernityscotland comment

This is a really good answer. Why?

First of all, it really answers the question. This isn't a pre-prepared answer. Look at how it uses phrases from the question, like "income" and "health" all the way through the essay.

It is balanced too. It doesn't just give one point of view. It has a debate, explaining that there are several reasons for the link between income and health. It's not simplistic.

There are four really well made points. There isn't a lot of statistics and the few that are used are quite broad, but they're accurate. Glasgow is often used as an example of poverty, but this was a specific area of Glasgow, which is a relevant one. People from Easterhouse in Glasgow, which is a low income area, have the highest rates of smoking in the UK. But it also notes that other parts of Scotland have poverty and wealth too.

Really good answers should have conclusions all the way through the answer, rather than a "conclusion" at the end, which is often a summing up, rather than a genuine conclusion. This answer draws conclusions through the essay. *"Health is not just physical health, its mental health too"*. That's a great conclusion! *"There has to be a better reason to explain the link between income and health"*. That's great too.

The references to Dr Harry Burns is really good to see and highly relevant. Binge drinking is growing, among women especially, in all social classes. Obesity is a problem for all social classes. The pressure to buy junk food may be greater for low income groups, but many young people from well off backgrounds choose unhealthy eating and drinking habits too. But health inequalities remain. This essay tries to explain this.

Remember, this essay was written in 22 minutes. There is a limit to how much you can write in 22 minutes. Everyone else is in the same boat. So, if you feel an essay you write in 22 minutes isn't your best one, don't be down-hearted. It's the same for everyone. If you answer the question in a balanced way, with some good, relevant, up to date examples, you'll be just fine.

Answering Paper Two Decision Making Exercise

You have 75 minutes for this paper.

First, you have to answer short questions based on textual and statistical sources provided. These are worth 10 marks.

Second, you have to write a Decision Making Exercise (DME) report based on textual and statistical sources provided. Recalled background knowledge must be provided too. The DME is worth 20 marks.

The DME will be on an aspect of Social Issues in the UK.

You will be presented with an issue, for example, whether or not to charge for appointments at a GP surgery.

A large textual Source will set out reasons why this should happen.

A large textual Source will set out reasons why it should not happen.

You need to make a decision, explain your reasons and comment on opposing reasons.

You need to use the textual sources, all the statistical sources and add your own relevant background knowledge to the report which is not contained in any of the sources provided.

Given all you said about time management in Paper One, is there any advice for Paper Two?

There is not the same pressure of time with Paper Two as there is with Paper One, but you still need to manage your time.

Think about the following time allocation:

    25 minutes to do the short questions

    15 minutes to make up a DME plan

    35 minutes to write the DME report

How do I get the best marks for the short questions?

Again, practice though makes perfect. There is no excuse for getting less than 7/10 for the short questions.

You are throwing away a good grade by getting anything less.

Always look at the statistical sources in the question first.

For example;

In Questions 1 to 3, use only the Sources described in each question.

Question 1

Use only Source C1, Source C2 and Source A.

To what extent does the evidence support the view of Roddy Frame? (3)

Look at the statistical Sources, C1 and C2, first and you'll have an idea what Roddy Frame is on about.

Always use the full quotation in your answer.

Your answer should go straight to the point. For example:

> *Roddy Frame says, "Life expectancy continues to rise year on year. Men in the UK, in particular, now have the highest life expectancy anywhere in the EU". Source C1 shows he is correct as life expectancy has risen for males and females since 1983-85. But he is incorrect with regard to Source C2 as male life expectancy for men in the UK is not the highest compared to other EU countries.*

This answer would get the full 3/3 marks.

Once you adopt this technique, there is no reason why you cannot get every short question completely correct.

Do I need headings in my report?

It's certainly a very good idea. Your DME should read like a report. It is different from the essays you write in paper one.

Reports usually have headings, so make sure you have headings. Underlining your headings with a ruler makes your headings stand out, though, of course, using a ruler is not compulsory.

Can any of the two options be correct?

Yes

What if I think one option is complete rubbish, do I need to write a balanced answer?

Yes, you do need to write a balanced answer. Even if you think an option is very wrong, do not rubbish it. You must state 4 or 5 good reasons for your case.

You should then comment on why the other viewpoint has some validity. It will have. You might not agree with it, but there will be sensible reasons why someone would argue this case.

How many points should I make?

Four or five well argued points are sufficient.

Take a wee look at the long textual sources. They will have four or five paragraphs which all have an argument contained within them. Use these sources to develop your arguments.

Do not copy the text though. This has to be your work and you have to explain your arguments in your own words.

What's this "rebuttal" thing my teacher is on about?

What you need to do in the DME is make a decision and justify it in a balanced way.

If your decision is too balanced, and you explain the reasons against your decision as well as the reasons for it, you're not being particularly decisive.

So, it's always good practice to "rebut" opposing views. This means that you explain why your point of view is better than the opposing one.

There is no set way to do this. You can have a heading called "rebuttal" or you can just rebut each opposing point one at a time.

I'm hopeless at background knowledge (BK). Is it right that I'll fail this task if I don't have any? If so, how can I make sure I get BK in my report.

Yes, if your report has no BK, the most you can get for this task is 9/20.

Hoping that you'll remember BK on the day is no use. You must prepare, even though you have no idea what the specific task will be on.

You do, however, know that it will be on some aspect of UK Social Issues, so why not prepare some good examples of relevant back ground knowledge?

Mnemonics are a good idea.

Let's say your name is Megan:

M stands for ... More Choices More ChancE stands for ... Equality Act

G stands for ... Government policy on health inequalities

A stands for ... Asylum seekers

N stands for ... National Minimum Wage

There is a full A-Z of chunks of background knowledge at the end of this article.

Write your chosen chunks down as soon as you get into the exam hall. Depending on the task, you could potentially have several very good pieces of BK ready to insert throughout your report.

So, I can just bung in all these chunks of BK into my report?

No!

Your BK must be relevant to the task. Say, for example, the DME task was on whether or not to introduce charges for visiting the doctor, knowing about G (Government policies on health inequalities) would be great BK.

But E (the Equality Act) might be a bit artificial and contrived. Having chunks of BK interspersed throughout the report is always the best style to adopt. This makes your report flow and sound as if you really know your social issues.

If I don't know any BK can I just make it up? Surely the markers won't know what goes on in my local area?

Your BK has to be relevant and also in the public domain. That is, it must be something which actually exists or has happened in the real world. If it's a local hospital in your area that has closed and that's relevant to the task, great, add it to your report.

On the other hand, if your neighbour next door is a benefit fraudster (unless he/she has been in the media for this crime) then providing that information would not be good BK.

Model Answer Decision Making Exercise

Task: You are the Minister for Work and Pensions. You have to decide whether or not to means-test Child Benefit.

Introduction

There are many relevant arguments for and against the means-testing of child benefit. I am going to recommend the proposal of introducing means-testing of child benefit.

> *Modernityscotland comment: This is good. State your decision right at the start.*

Arguments For

It is not necessary to give all families with children child benefit. As James Grant points out in Source A, there are many families in the UK who do not need this payment every week. It would be more beneficial to stop payment to those who do not need it. This would mean that tax payers' money could be spent elsewhere, where it is needed more urgently. The Coalition Government has suggested stopping child benefit for those who earn over £42,000 per year (BK) and this seems to me to make sense. There must be more deserving cases than those who earn £42,000 per year

Source C2 shows us that we have one of the highest percentages of children in Europe living in poverty; 25%. This is a clear indication that there are many children who also need this benefit more than others do. If means-testing was introduced, we would not pay much needed funds to the 75% of families who do not need it. We could increase benefits to those who do need it and therefore cut child poverty in the UK.

Source C3 shows that child benefit is the third highest pay out of benefits with an annual cost of £9.8 billion. This figure could be cut dramatically if means-testing was introduced, thus giving the government more money to put to more pressing benefits such as Incapacity Benefit.

Source C2 shows that the number of people living in poverty has increased (to 3.8 million) for the first time in a decade. This means that there will be more demand for other benefits such as Incapacity benefit and Income support. If means-testing was introduced, this would give the government more money to put into providing benefits for the growing numbers living in poverty.

James Grant is right. Other countries, such as Australia and Canada already have taken the means-testing approach, with great success. In these countries child benefit is only paid to those living in poverty.

> *Modernityscotland comment: It is always a good idea to highlight the sources you use, as well as your BK. This answer has used Sources C1, C2 and C3. It has taken some of the main points of James Grant too, to construct strong arguments for the decision.*

> *You don't necessarily have to use these headings. You can make up your own if you want. So long as you follow the instructions for the task.*

Arguments Against

Trisha Yearwood claims that the money that could be saved by introducing means-testing could just be wasted in administration costs that would occur if every family in the UK were to be means-tested. New Labour introduced a lot of means-tested benefits, such as the Working Tax Credit (BK). Many of these were not taken up because the forms were too complicated. Millions of pounds were paid to the wrong people! (BK)

The SNP Scottish Government has promised to bring in free school meals for all children in P1-P3 (BK). This could cost £50 million. But, obesity is a big problem in the UK (BK). If we spend now, we could save money in the long term. Source C3 shows that the percentage of children living in poverty has fallen in all areas of the UK. Some people believe that this is due to the current policies on benefits and these should not change. Perhaps if we were to increase means-testing these figures would begin to rise again.

Source C1 shows that Britain already has one of the lowest percentages of social welfare spending; 21.8%. The Government has been able to find billions for the war in Iraq (BK) and in bailing out the banks! (BK) If it can help well off bankers, it can find money to make sure our children are properly looked after.

Trisha Yearwood claims that means testing child benefit could widen inequalities. Too many children do not get the start in life they deserve. The gap between the very rich and the poor increased during the New Labour years (BK).

Modernityscotland comment: The opposing view is a reasonable one. It makes sense. Don't dismiss it. Present the main objections to your decision, don't avoid them. This answer does this well. And it keeps using the sources, bringing in good BK as well.

Rebuttal

There has been money wasted on administration costs. But the Government has learned from its mistakes. Costs will reduce once the system is up and running, ensuring that those who really need the money get it, while we are no longer wasting money paying child benefit to the well off. There are some genuine people who haven't claimed, but we could cut down on fraudulent claims, as the tough rules put off bogus claimants.

It is always popular to give out benefits to children, but if we really look at who would be getting the money, I feel the money could be better spent elsewhere. Those who are genuinely living in poverty will still receive it, means-testing or no means-testing.

In fact, those who are genuinely in need may receive more help. We have a major problem in Scotland with NEETs (BK). The money saved on universal child benefits could be invested in early years help for children from poor backgrounds. The Scottish Government through its Equally Well programme (BK) has made this a priority.

While what Source C1 says is true, we still have one of the highest percentages of children living in poverty. There seems to be a connection over how much you spend on benefits and the number of children living in poverty. For example, Sweden spends 28.9% of its GDP and only 8.8% of children living in poverty. Compare this to our 21.8% of spending and the subsequent 25% of children living in poverty.

Trisha Yearwood is wrong when she says that means-testing would increase wealth inequalities. Instead it would target money towards the poorest, rather than the richest as the present system does.

Modernityscotland comment: These are good rebuttal arguments, which show decisive, yet balanced comments. Again, notice how BK is interspersed throughout the report, even the rebuttal section.

Concluding Comments

While the arguments put forward against means-testing have some substance, I believe those in favour of introducing means-testing have the decisive arguments. As James Grant puts it, the Government cannot continue to go on paying money to people regardless of their income or savings. So, it would be more beneficial to introduce means-testing for child benefit.

Modernityscotland comment: this is an impressive answer. It does all it has been asked to do. This report shows evidence of sound planning. This is a top A pass.

Background Knowledge: An A to Z

Let's be clear about background knowledge. It has to be relevant to the arguments in the DME. It has to be real knowledge of real issues in the public domain.

Here are 26 examples of background knowledge. You may well know many more. But, at least, these examples give you something to go on.

However, be careful. Depending on the decision you have to make, some of these may well be inappropriate or irrelevant. It's up to you to decide, based on the topic of the report you have to write.

A is for Attitudes

The 2010 British Social Attitudes Survey showed the British people to have mixed views towards spending on social issues.

On the one hand, there was a move to the Right, with fewer people (27%) believing that Government should spend more on benefits. Only 36% believed that Government should redistribute income towards the poor.

On the other hand, the majority of people are happy with state spending on health and education. 64% of the public are happy with the way the NHS is run and 73% are happy with the teaching of basic skills.

B is for Barnett Formula

Currently, the Scottish Parliament does not raise any of its own finances. It could vary income tax by up to 3p in the £ but has chosen not to.

Westminster's so-called Barnett Formula decides how much money the Scottish Parliament receives. The Scottish National Party would like to see Scotland become completely independent from the rest of the UK and would like greater "fiscal autonomy" as a step towards independence.

The Coalition Government has published the Scotland Bill, which could, if passed by Parliament, amend the Barnett Formula and give the Scottish Parliament greater tax raising powers.

C is for Commonwealth Games

The 2014 Glasgow Commonwealth Games is having a major impact on the east end of Glasgow, an area which, for some time, has been associated with a variety of social problems.

The Athletes' Village is just one example. Following the Games, the Athletes' Village will be developed to become an attractive residential area, comprising a total of 1,400 homes, 300 of which will be available for social rental. Lessons, we have been told, have been learned from previous Glasgow housing developments. This time, social amenities, such as parks, sporting and shopping facilities will be created. The east end (see D for Deprivation) could be transformed.

D is for Deprivation

Deprivation means that individuals and communities are deprived of the things which make up a good quality of life. Unemployment and bad housing are the key drivers of deprivation. These have consequences of crime, drug and alcohol abuse, poor health and low educational attainment. The 2009 Scottish Index of Multiple Deprivation study showed that the ten most deprived areas in Scotland are located within Glasgow City and Renfrewshire. Edinburgh and the north-east region have seven of the ten least deprived communities.

Top 10 most deprived areas (Based on post codes):
1. Parkhead West and Barrowfield, Glasgow
2. Paisley Ferguslie, Renfrewshire
3. Keppochhill, Glasgow
4. Possilpark, Glasgow

5. Glenwood North, Glasgow
6. Possilpark, Glasgow
7. Parkhead West and Barrowfield, Glasgow
8. Paisley Ferguslie, Renfrewshire
9. Paisley Ferguslie, Renfrewshire
10. Drumchapel North, Glasgow

Top 10 least deprived:
1. Banchory, Aberdeenshire
2. Craiglockhart, Edinburgh
3. Lower Whitecraigs and South Giffnock, East Renfrewshire
4. Morningside, Edinburgh
5. Stockbridge, Edinburgh
6. Merrylee and Braidbar, East Renfrewshire
7. Midstocket, Aberdeen
8. Whitecraigs and Broom, East Renfrewshire
9. Marchmont West, Edinburgh
10. Comely Bank, Edinburgh

E is for Equal Pay

In 2003, the Equal Pay Act was amended. The most obvious feature of the act is that women must be paid the same as men for the jobs that they do. But, the devil of the law is always in the detail.

Women must be paid the same as men for a job of "equal value", not just the same job. For example, local authority cleaners are usually women. Local authority waste disposal officers ("bin men") are more likely to be male. But, over the years the bin men have been paid much more than the cleaners.

Now it's payback time. Successful back dated claims by trade unions and "no-win-no-fee" lawyers, are now costing Scottish local authorities millions. There have been 35,000 equal pay claims made in Scotland and the settlements could come to as much as £1 billion

F is for Female high flyers

Just some women who have broken through the glass ceiling in their profession; Kirsty Wark, presenter of BBC Newsnight, Elish

Angiolini, the Lord Advocate for Scotland, Scotland's top lawyer, Professor Joan Stringer, head of Napier University, Edinburgh, Heather Graham, first Chief Police Officer in Scotland (Fife Constabulary). In the private sector, Michelle Mone is the co-owner of MJM International and creator of Ultimo, the UK's leading designer lingerie brand.

G is for Glass Ceiling
Gender discrimination is against the law.

But, women remain very unequal to men. Some statistics; In Scotland, women make up 31.3% of MSPs, 20.9% of secondary head-teachers, 18.8% of local authority leaders, 12.5% of local authority leaders, 11.8% of senior judges, 11.6% of senior police officers.

In the UK, women make up 19.5 % of MPs, 17.4% of newspaper editors, 10.4% of directors of the top 100 companies.

At the current rate of progress, it would take women another 200 years to reach equality with men in terms of numbers of MPs. It would take 60 years to equal men in directors of top 100 companies and 40 years to equal the number of male senior judges.

H is for Harry Burns
Dr Harry Burns is the Chief Medical officer for Scotland and the Scottish Government's leading health advisor. His "biology of poverty" research argues that the key to narrowing health inequalities is to intervene as early as possible in the lives of at-risk children. He believes that health problems start at the very beginning of life and that a "chaotic" upbringing results in health problems and, ultimately, premature death.

I is for Iraq
The UK's Iraq Inquiry in January 2010 showed that war in Iraq has cost the British tax payer £9.24billion.

There will be other, significant, costs to the NHS. Thousands of British troops in Iraq have been identified with mental health problems. There have been over 300 cases of Post Traumatic Stress Disorder.

J is for Jobseekers Allowance

Officially, there is no such benefit as unemployment benefit. Those out of work may, instead, be entitled to Jobseekers Allowance (JSA).

The language is important. The Government wants the mindset of those out of work to be that of active job seekers, rather than passive claimants of benefits. The amount of JSA paid by the Social Security Agency depends on individual circumstances, but it is normally between £50-70 per week for single people.

If you're still out of work after six months, you'll be asked to attend a 'restart interview'. Depending on your age and situation, you may change to another scheme, such as the New Deal. In December 2010, there were 1.46 million people in the UK claiming JSA.

K is for Kensington

K is for Kensington. The highest life expectancy in the UK is to be found in Kensington and Chelsea (London).

Average female life expectancy is 86.2 years, average male life expectancy is 82.2 years. The lowest life expectancy is found in Glasgow Shettleston, where average female life expectancy is just 76.7 years and average male life expectancy just 69.9 years. Males in Glasgow Shettleston have a lower life expectancy than men in Algeria, Egypt, Turkey and Vietnam.

L is for Lifestyle choices

Not all poor people have bad diets. Not all well off people live healthy lives.

Pete Doherty is a very well-off rock star. Yet he has, in the past made, shall we agree, unwise lifestyle choices?

Taking drugs is a lifestyle choice. Smoking is a lifestyle choice. Eating chips is a lifestyle choice. Surely everyone today knows these things are bad for your health?

Taking exercise is a lifestyle choice. Eating fruit and drinking water are lifestyle choices too. Surely everyone today knows these things are good for your health?

The link between wealth and health is very strong. But at the end of the day, individuals make good or bad lifestyle decisions.

However, it is easier for some people to make good choices than it is for others.

M is for Minimum Wage

The Labour Government of 1997-2001 introduced the National Minimum Wage (NMW). The NMW, from October 2010, is £5.93 per hour for those 21 and over, £4.92 for those aged between 18 and 20 and £3.64 for 16-17 year olds.

N is for NEETS

"NEETs" is the term used to describe young people who are Not in Education, Employment or Training. Currently there are around 15,000 teenage NEETs in Scotland. NEETS are much more likely to be socially excluded and involved in crime.

The SNP Government does not use the term NEETS any longer, arguing that the term has "negative connotations". Instead the Scottish Government refers to the "More Choices, More Chances" group.

Research for the Scottish Government has shown that the Educational Maintenance Allowance scheme (EMA), whereby pupils from lower income families receive benefit to stay on at school, is not improving the educational attainment of NEETs. It found that most who claim EMA would stay on at school anyway and NEETS are not staying on at school for Highers.

Glasgow City Council runs a vocational training programme for the entire west of Scotland. This has proved to be successful in improving truancy and behaviour, as well as job prospects.

O is for Ownership

Property ownership in Scotland has more than doubled in the last 30 years.

Nearly two thirds of homes are now owner-occupied, compared with a figure of just over 30 per cent in 1970. 63% of Scottish households are owner-occupiers. 29% are social renters (from a local authority or housing association). 6% rent from a private landlord.

Home ownership has grown partly because of Right to Buy legislation. This is a policy introduced by the Conservatives that allowed individuals living in council houses to buy their rented home at a discounted price. There has been a decline in the number of local authority houses available for rent, which has forced people to take out mortgages to buy homes.

But, the credit crunch has meant that many people who over-stretched themselves to borrow are now in financial trouble. Many young people now cannot get a mortgage at all. This has led to a boom in the rental market.

The Scottish Government seeks to close the gap in housing inequalities. It supports the Homestake scheme, in which the owner only pays a fraction of the house price, and the remainder is paid by a social landlord, such as a housing association.

P is for Poverty
In March 2007, a unique five year study of poverty was published.

The Child Poverty Action Group, the Poverty Alliance, as well as academics from the country's top universities, reported their findings.

It found that in 1979, only one in eight children lived in poverty, one in five of the Scottish population. 910,000 people live in poverty, one in four Scottish children. 240,000 boys and girls live in poverty. One in five poor people live in Glasgow. One in ten of Scotland's rural population is officially poor.

Overall, there is now more poverty in Scotland in the 21st century than there was in the 1960s.

Q is for the Queen
The Sunday Times newspaper publishes its Rich List every year.

The 2010 Rich List showed that the Queen, who traditionally used to be the richest person in the UK, is not any more. Not by a long way.

With assets of £290 million, she is only the 245th richest person in the UKThe steel tycoon, Lakhsmi Mittal, is Britain's richest man, with assets worth £22.45 billion. Chelsea owner, Ramon Abramovich, is second with £7.4 billion.

A global study, from the World Institute for Development

Economics Research of the United Nations, found that the richest 1% of adults in the world own 40% of the planet's wealth. The report found the richest 10% of adults accounted for 85% of the world total of global assets. Half the world's adult population, however, own barely 1% of global wealth between them.

R is for Raploch

The Raploch council estate in Stirling is a classic case of a poor community which is now benefiting from investment by a variety of public and private organisations.

For years the Raploch had all the vices of any poor state in Scotland. There was high unemployment, poor health and high rates of crime. The anti-social behaviour of one Mags Haney brought national attention to the estate and not for the right reasons.

Now, through "joined up" or partnership working by the Scottish Government, NHS Scotland and Scottish Enterprise, life in the Raploch is improving for its residents. Housing has improved. There is lower crime and drug abuse. There is still poverty, but a combination of collectivism (government action) and individual responsibility has created success stories.

S is for Scottish Parliament

Since 1999, the Scottish Parliament has assumed powers over many areas of our day to day life. These include education, health, housing, criminal justice and the environment.

The 2006 ban on smoking in enclosed public spaces has, perhaps, been the most high profile of the Scottish Parliament's laws. Scotland does not have graduate tuition fees, but England does. Students from England who study in Scotland have to pay fees, as do students from Scotland who study in England.

T is for Taxation

We are taxed on just about everything we earn and everything we spend.

Incomes are taxed by Income Tax. Businesses pay Corporation tax. Savings are taxed. Spending is taxed too. If you buy a house you are likely to pay "Stamp Duty". Car owners pay Road Tax.

Most goods we buy in the shops are subject to Value Added Tax. For most people in the UK, a large part of their earnings go towards Council Tax. Even when we die, many people's assets are subject to Inheritance Tax.

Tax can be used to create more, or less equality. The Chancellor's changes affect everyone differently, depending on individual financial circumstances and spending choices.

The most recent changes in UK Income Tax came into effect in June 2010. Those earning £0 – £2,044 pay 10% in Income Tax. £0 – £37,400 pay the standard rate of 20%. Those earning £37,401 start to pay the Higher rate, of 40%. Those earning over £150,000 pay 50%. All are subject to personal allowances, which are not taxable.

U is for Universal Benefits

A universal benefit is available equally to all people and is not means tested. On the other hand, a means-tested benefit is something a person receives only once their income has been taken into account.

A good example of a universal benefit is, or was, Child Benefit. Currently all parents in the UK receive child benefit for their children, regardless of income.

Parents receive £20.30 per week for the first child and £13.40 per week for others. But, from 2014, under Coalition Government plans, Child Benefit will be means-tested for the first time. Higher rate taxpayers, estimated to be those earning over £42,000 will receive no Child Benefit at all. Ironically, a two-income family with a joint income of £83,000, with both parents earning £41,500 each, would continue to receive Child Benefit.

A good example of a means tested benefit is free school meals. Only those parents who are unemployed, or on low incomes, are entitled to free school meals.

Currently, around 122,000 children in Scotland receive free school meals. The former Labour Government in Westminster preferred means tested to universal benefits. However, the SNP Scottish Government prefers universal benefits.

In April 2008 it started phasing out prescription charges for everyone. The Scottish Government has piloted a free school meals for all scheme in deprived areas.

V is for Vulnerable.

Perhaps the most vulnerable in our society are the elderly.

The 2007 report by the Care Commission found that many elderly people in Scotland's residential care homes are malnourished and dehydrated. Two-thirds of institutions are failing to meet basic standards of health and welfare. More than 6000 people living in residential homes for the elderly in Scotland are still sharing a room.

More than half of all the complaints made to the Care Commission were against care homes for older people.

W is for Welfare Reform

The Coalition Government has promised a "welfare revolution".

Work and pensions Secretary Iain Duncan Smith has pledged to abolish all the various, complicated, benefits and tax credits. In their place, he proposes a "universal credit". The Minister insists that about 2.5 million of the poorest people will actually see their income rise.

Iain Duncan Smith has gone further and bolder than New Labour, which also tried to reform welfare.

At present, those on Jobseekers Allowance (JSA) who refuse a job can lose their JSA payments, currently £64.45 a week for most people, for up to 26 weeks.

Under the new plans, if Jobseekers Allowance claimants refuse a job, or do not agree to do community work, they will lose the benefit for three months. After a second refusal of work, they will lose it for six months. If they refuse a job for the third time, they will lose the benefit for three years.

The Coalition Government also plans to introduce a Proposal Test to decide whether current sick and disabled claimants are capable of some kind of work. The Coalition Government proposes a £400-a-week cap on Housing Benefits from April 2011.

X is for Xenophobia

Xenophobia literally means fear of foreigners. Asylum seekers living in Scotland have been the victims of xenophobic attacks.

Racist attacks are a serious problem in Scotland. The number of racist incidents recorded by Scottish Police Forces in 2007-8 stood at 5,243. People of Pakistani origin were most likely to be the victim of a racist incident, with 1654 cases across Scotland, accounting for one-third of all cases.

Y is for Young Scot awards

Young people often make headlines for negative reasons.

But it is a minority of young Scots, just as it is a minority of older Scots, who indulge in anti-social behaviour. Each year, Young Scot and the Sunday Mail newspaper acknowledge the many positive things achieved by young people across Scotland. In 2010, footballer Islam Feruz won the award.

Z is for Zero Tolerance

Zero Tolerance is when the Government and legal system take a hard line on every case of anti-social behaviour. In 2009, the Scottish Parliament passed The Offences (Aggravation by Prejudice) (Scotland) Act.

The Act creates aggravations, similar to those which exist for race and religion hate crime, for crimes motivated by prejudice relating to disability, sexual orientation and transgender status. It means that courts, when sentencing crimes "motivated by malice or ill-will" based on a victim's actual or presumed sexual orientation, transgender identity or disability, must take into account the motivation for the offence. This may then result in an alternative or a more severe sentence.

POLITICAL ISSUES
IN THE UK

Study Theme 1A Devolved Decision Making in Scotland

Need to know

➤ Powers of the Scottish Parliament
➤ Decision Making in the Scottish Parliament
➤ How Scotland is represented at Westminster
➤ Relations between the Scottish Parliament and Westminster
➤ Powers of Scottish local government
➤ How Local Government is funded
➤ Relations between Scottish local government and the Scottish Parliament
➤ Arguments for reform of Local Government
➤ Effects of Single Transferable Voting System (STV) on decision making

What powers does the Scottish Parliament have?

Even though there is a Scottish Parliament, and the SNP is in charge of the Scottish Government, Scotland is NOT an independent country.

Scotland is not a "sovereign" nation with control over its own borders and the protection of those borders. Scotland remains part of the United Kingdom of Scotland, England, Wales and Northern Ireland. People entitled to live in Scotland are citizens of the United Kingdom.

The following "devolved powers" are the areas of law the Scottish Parliament has authority over: Agriculture, Forestry and Fishing, Economic Development, Education, Environment, Health, Housing, Justice and the Legal System, Local Government, Natural and Built Heritage, Police and Fire Services, Planning, Social Work, Public Registers and Records, some Transport, Sport and the Arts, and Tourism

Reserved Matters are issues where the power to make laws has been kept by the UK Parliament at Westminster in London.

Some examples are: Constitutional Matters, Abortion, Broadcasting/Entertainment Data Protection, Defence, Drug Laws, Employment Law, Elections, Equal Opportunities, Energy – coal, gas, oil, electricity and nuclear energy, Foreign Policy, Gambling and National Lottery, Guns and Weapons, Social Security, Some Transport, Trade and Industry, UK National Security.

Surely some of the powers overlap?

They do. Take immigration, for example, which is a Reserved power.

The UK Government decides immigration policy.

The UK Home Office decides, for example, on which asylum seekers living in Scotland, are allowed to stay in Scotland. But, Scotland will be the home for some who seek asylum in the UK. X Factor singer Gamu Nhengu and her family, for example.

It is Scottish local authorities' education, housing and social work departments who will look after asylum seekers. Gamu lived and went to school in Clackmannanshire. But the UK Home Office ultimately decides who stays in and who leaves Scotland.

Foreign Policy and Justice overlap too. Foreign Policy is a UK power. But, Justice is a devolved power, and decisions made by Scotland's Justice Secretary can have a major impact on UK foreign policy.

In August 2009, Scottish Justice Secretary Kenny Macaskill released convicted Lockerbie bomber Abdelbaset Ali al-Megrahi, on compassionate grounds. He was diagnosed as having terminal cancer, with an expected three months to live. This decision upset the USA Government and damaged UK relations with the USA.

Is the Scottish Parliament likely to get any more powers?

The SNP would, of course, like the Scottish Parliament to have control over as many powers as possible, ultimately to become fully independent by gaining the reserved powers from Westminster. The Scottish Greens also support Scottish independence.

The "Unionist" parties; Scottish Conservatives, Scottish Labour and Scottish Liberal Democrats oppose Scottish independence.

In 2007, First Minister Alex Salmond launched the "National Conversation" to assess public support for independence. The Unionist parties responded by asking Sir Kenneth Calman and his commission to see if the Scottish Parliament could have additional powers within the UK.

The Calman Commission recommended that the Scottish Parliament be given new powers; It recommended that the UK Treasury should cut income tax by 10p in the £ for all workers in Scotland but that the block grant to Scotland also be cut. Calman would like the Scottish Government to tax the Scottish people to meet any shortfall.

Calman also supported more powers over air guns, drink driving and the speed limit.

It remains to be seen whether the Westminster Coalition Government will implement all of the recommendations of Calman.

In November 2010, the UK Coalition Government published its Scotland Bill.

If passed by the House of Commons, it would give the Scottish Parliament control over a proportion of the income tax revenue raised in Scotland, Stamp Duty and Landfill Tax. The Scottish Parliament would also gain the power to set national speed limits, drink-driving laws and legislation on the control of airguns.

The block grant, governed by the Barnett Formula from Westminster would continue. But, it will be cut. In return, the Scottish Government will be given control over half of the amount raised in income tax within Scotland.

The Scottish Parliament would be granted important new borrowing powers to fund major new capital projects.

What differences has the Scottish Parliament made?

Since devolution, Scottish Governments have introduced laws and policies which are very different from the rest of the UK.

Scottish students at Scottish universities do not pay any tuition fees for their first degree. The situation is very different in England where a university degree could soon, in theory, cost £9,000 per year.

Prescription charges in Scotland will be abolished in April 2011. Those in England who are not exempt from prescription charges will still have to pay.

Who holds power in the Scottish Parliament?

There are 129 Members of the Scottish Parliament (MSPs).

MSPs are elected using the Additional Member System (AMS). Under the AMS, 73 MSPs are constituency MSPS, and 56 are Regional list MSPs. The AMS makes it very difficult for any one party to have a majority over all the other parties.

It is not, of course, impossible, but in recent times both Scottish Labour and the SNP have normally polled around 30% of the vote, meaning that, in all probability, power will be shared. There will either be a coalition government, as there was between 1999-2007 with Scottish Labour and the Scottish Liberal Democrats sharing power. Or there will be a minority Government, as we have had with the SNP government since the 2007 elections.

The SNP has 47 MSPs and is the largest party. This means that the Scottish Government has had to pass its legislation on an "issue by issue" basis. But it is in the minority and can be defeated, if sufficient MSPs from the other parties vote against it!

Any examples of this?

The SNP Scottish Government was defeated almost right away when the Parliament voted not to abolish the Edinburgh tram project. More recently, the Scottish Government was defeated when it tried to set minimum prices for alcohol.

Lack of parliamentary support meant that the Scottish Government abandoned its election commitments to abolish the Council Tax and have a referendum on Scottish independence.

Are there any other ways MSPs or outside groups can influence decision making?

The Scottish Government is held accountable in a number of ways.

Firstly, the First Minister and the Cabinet Secretaries have to account for their actions both at First Ministers Questions and

Question Time. Labour First Minister Henry McLeish was forced to resign after he was quizzed at First Minister's Question time over improper use of his constituency office. In November 2010, Cabinet Secretary John Swinney had to apologise to the Scottish Parliament at Question Time for not revealing that the "tartan tax" had lapsed.

Secondly, it is important to recognise that much of what goes on in the Scottish Parliament chamber is theatrics. MSPs who indulge in party political point scoring in the chamber will work quite productively with each other in the Scottish Parliament's various committees. The Scottish Parliament has a number of mandatory and subject committees. Scottish Parliament committees frequently consult the public when conducting inquiries into issues of concern or considering the general principles of a bill. These committees do not just review and scrutinise legislation but can propose legislation too.

Thirdly, Cross-Party Groups (CPGs) provide an opportunity for MSPs of all parties, outside organisations and members of the public to meet and discuss a shared interest in a particular cause or subject.

Fourthly, MSPs can try to have a Member's Bill passed. Here, the MSP or an outside body takes responsibility for gaining parliamentary support for a particular issue. In 2009, Green MSP Patrick Harvie succeeded in having The Offences (Aggravation by Prejudice) (Scotland) Act passed by the Scottish Parliament.

Lastly, Scottish citizens can use the Scottish Parliament's Petitions Committee to try and have a bill passed on an issue which concerns them. Any person or group may submit a petition to the Scottish Parliament. In 2008, Kenny Shand raised a petition in the Scottish Parliament highlighting the problems faced by disabled drivers when able-bodied drivers leave their cars in their parking spaces. The Disabled Persons' Parking Places (Scotland) Act 2009 became law on October 1 2009.

What is the point of having MPs if all the important things to do with Scotland are decided by the Scottish Parliament?

Remember that many important powers concerning people living in Scotland are still decided at Westminster. These include issues such as social security and defence.

Scotland is represented at Westminster by the 59 MPs elected from Scottish constituencies. Only one of these MPs is a Conservative, but there are 11 Liberal Democrat MPs from Scottish constituencies, providing the UK Coalition Government with a greater Scottish presence.

Scotland is represented in the Cabinet by the Secretary of State for Scotland, currently Michael Moore MP (Liberal Democrat). He heads the Scotland Office, whose main roles are to represent Scottish interests within the UK Government and manage the devolution settlement.

The Scottish Affairs Committee is a Commons committee comprised of eleven MPs appointed by the House of Commons to examine the expenditure, administration and policy of the Scotland Office.

Some believe that the Scotland Office, far from "oiling the wheels of devolution", is now unnecessary. The SNP believes that its running costs of over £7 million per year are too high and that the office should be scrapped.

The SNP would say that though, wouldn't they?

Of course! The SNP would like the Scottish Parliament to be completely independent from Westminster. The job of the Scotland Office is to make sure that the Scottish Parliament and the Westminster Parliament work together.

What are relations like between the Scottish Parliament and Westminster?

Relations were obviously easier when Labour was in control at Westminster and the major party in the Scottish Parliament. Labour introduced devolution and Scottish Labour is strongly committed to the UK.

By contrast, the whole point of the SNP being in government is to make Scotland independent. Perhaps not today or tomorrow, but at some point. So, while Alex Salmond will co-operate with the UK Government on some things, perhaps confrontation is inevitable.

David Cameron stated that he wanted a "fresh start" with the Scottish Parliament. He visited the Scottish Parliament just days after becoming Prime Minister. The "respect agenda" is designed to ensure that both Governments work with each other as much as possible.

The "respect agenda" has been strained by the rows over released Lockerbie bomber Abdelbaset Ali al-Megrahi, with David Cameron criticising the Scottish Government whilst in the USA.

Likewise, the Scottish Government is not best pleased about the decision taken by the Westminster Government to hold the referendum on the UK voting system on the same day as the 2011 Scottish parliament elections.

The Scottish Government has been highly critical of Chancellor George Osborne's budget cuts, stating that Scotland, which has a large public sector, will be impacted worse than other areas of the UK. Moray's RAF bases at Kinloss and Lossiemouth are at risk due to defence cuts.

How is the Scottish Parliament Funded?

The Scottish Parliament is funded from the UK Government at Westminster. In 2010, its budget was £35 billion. This figure takes the form of a "block grant", worked out by the "Barnett Formula". In theory, the Scottish Parliament could raise an additional 3p in the pound in direct taxation via the so-called "tartan tax". The Scottish Parliament has yet to use the tartan tax. Indeed, in November 2010 it was revealed that the tax power had "lapsed" and that it would cost the Scottish Government £7m to have it restored.

How do the English feel about Scotland having, for example, no tuition fees, yet Scotland won't raise the "tartan tax" to pay for it? The block grant is controversial. The SNP would like Scotland to raise all of its own taxation. This is referred to as "fiscal autonomy". The Unionist parties are opposed to this.

Some MPs from English constituencies resent the "interference" of MPs from Scotland in matters that have been devolved to the Scottish Parliament. This has become known as the "West Lothian Question". Their grievance is that MPs from Scotland can vote on, for example, English education or health issues in the UK Parliament but MPs from English constituencies have no control over Scottish education or health issues.

Arguments over the West Lothian Question came to a head

when the Blair Government passed the law on tuition fees for students going to English universities. Without the support of MPs from Scottish constituencies, it is unlikely the bill would have been passed.

Given that Scotland is likely to continue not to charge tuition fees and England's are likely to escalate, questions are likely to be asked why Scotland can afford not to charge and England cannot.

What does Local Government in Scotland do?

There are 32 Local Authorities (LAs) in Scotland. Many are very different, but others, particularly neighbouring ones, are very similar in size, composition and need. Scottish local government was organised into its current format in 1996 by the then UK Conservative Government.

The re-organisation was seen as a political ploy to break up Labour's control of large local authorities and create smaller, suburban, more affluent authorities, which would perhaps be more supportive of the Conservatives.

LAs in Scotland perform five very important roles:

Providing Services. For example, education, housing and social work, which are the most expensive services.

Strategic Planning. LAs, especially in these budget conscious times, have the job of making long term plans to improve services and provide best value.

Regulation. LAs regulate areas such as licensing of pubs, night clubs and taxi drivers.

Community leadership. LAs will lead campaigns, for example to promote tourism, healthy living or anti-litter strategies.

Local democracy. All LAs have elected representatives (councillors) who represent local people.

Where does local government get its money from?

The Scottish Government provides a block grant to LAs, which amounts to around 80% of its income with the remainder funded largely from local taxation such as Council Tax, Business Rates and charges for services.

Because the great bulk of LA funding comes from the Scottish

Government, the amount of money the Scottish Government has in its budget is vital.

The next few years are likely to see a decline in the size of the Scottish budget. In order to deal with the budget deficit, brought on by the bail-out of the banks, Chancellor George Osborne introduced an Emergency Budget in June 2010.

There will be annual cuts in Scottish public spending of around 4% for the next four to five years.

1 in 3 Scots works in the public sector. 95% of Scottish children go to state schools. Almost everyone in Scotland will be affected by the cuts.

Isn't the Council Tax being abolished?

Not yet. The SNP would like to abolish it but didn't have support in the Scottish Parliament.

It prefers a Local Income Tax, as do the Scottish Liberal Democrats, but the parties haven't been able to agree on a version of the tax.

As part of the "Concordat" agreement of 2007, Council Tax increases have been frozen. The SNP promises continued freezing of Council Tax rises if it is re-elected in 2011.

What is the Concordat?

The Concordat was agreed between the SNP Scottish Government and LA representatives' COSLA . It has resulted in:

The reduction of "ring fencing" of projects by the Scottish Government. LAs can now control much more of their budgets rather than being told by the Scottish Government what they have to spend it on. COSLA likes this.

The freezing of Council Tax increases. But, as budgets have been cut, COSLA would now like to raise more money for services by raising the Council Tax.

Single Outcome Agreements (SOAs). SOAs mean a focus on Inputs, Outputs and Outcomes. For example, in education, a SOA for a local authority means that it must focus on Inputs: More teachers, Outputs: Smaller class sizes and Outcomes: Successful learners, confident individuals, effective contributors and responsible citizens (The Curriculum for Excellence).

In the early days, COSLA was delighted with the Concordat. It gave local authorities much more power over how they spent their funds. It also served as an affirmation of their important role in Scottish life.

However, more recently, COSLA has become critical of the Concordat. As budgets have become tighter, some LA leaders would like the opportunity to increase Council Tax, but the Concordat will not allow this.

There have also been issues such as the lowering of P1 class sizes, an SNP election pledge. The SNP say that LAs have the funds to do this, COSLA claims they do not. Likewise, many LAs simply do not have the money to pay for free school meals in P1-P3, another Scottish Government aspiration.

If elected in May 2011, Scottish Labour would abolish the Concordat.

What about cuts in local government spending?

Many "efficiency savings" are being proposed. The average cut in Scottish LA budgets is 2.6%. The pressure to introduce cuts is straining relations between the Scottish Government and LAs. In 2010, Finance Secretary John Swinney forced through a Council Tax freeze for 2011-12 on the threat of even greater cuts, if LAs did not comply. City of Glasgow Council leader, Gordon Matheson, accused John Swinney of bullying and blackmail. He claimed that the Scottish Government's treatment of LAs was worse than "the darkest days of Tory rule".

John Swinney has pledged to protect Health spending. But this means that spending in other areas will be cut more. He also agreed with Westminster that the full budget cuts in Scotland would be delayed for one year. But, this could mean more severe cuts in years to come.

Across Scotland's 32 LAs there have been cuts in, for example, school transport, museums and sports centres, police overtime. Redundancies have been made and posts have remained unfilled. There have been increases in charges for school breakfast clubs, special refuse uplifts and blue badges for disabled drivers.

Do we need 32 different local authorities, with all the associated costs that are involved?

Many people are asking whether the current boundaries are

appropriate for the difficult financial times we are living in.

While the needs of a rural authority, such as Moray or Dumfries and Galloway, are obviously very different from the needs of Glasgow or Dundee, are LAs such as Clackmannanshire, Falkirk and Stirling so different? Could we not save a lot of money and administration costs if we had fewer LAs covering larger areas?

In November 2010, First Minister Alex Salmond launched a high-level commission to examine the future of local government, the health and emergency services and police forces. The redrawing of local government boundaries is likely to be explored.

Shared services have been cited as a potential route to cost savings and performance improvements for councils, and as such are being explored by almost every council.

In education, discussions have taken place between Midlothian and East Lothian councils in a bid to save money and improve standards within their education departments.

There are many small LAs within Scotland; the "three Ayrshires", for example, East, North and South, where many services could be provided together, making many efficiency savings.

How has the introduction of STV changed Scottish local authorities?

In 2007, the STV destroyed Labour's power base in Scottish local authorities. The SNP now has more local councillors than any other party.

Despite predictions of chaos and gridlock, STV has worked very well in Scottish local government. Coalition government is now the norm in Scotland. Parties who used to be sworn enemies of one another, now have to discuss and compromise on issues in a grown up manner.

South Lanarkshire and East Dunbartonshire Councils, for example, have a Labour/Conservative coalition, something which would have been unthinkable prior to devolution.

Voters can choose candidates within parties as well as between them. This has created real competition for seats. Councillors are having to work hard to maintain support and be re-elected, leading to better representation for the voter.

Study Theme 1B Decision Making in Central Government

Need to know

➤ Powers of the Prime Minister (PM) and Cabinet
➤ How Parliament can control the PM and Cabinet
➤ The role of senior civil servants
➤ The influence of pressure groups and the media on the UK Government

How powerful is the Prime Minister?

There is no one single formula for understanding PM power.

The PM's relationship with his Cabinet is usually referred to as "first among equals". He is the captain of the team. It is a team he has appointed and which he has certain certain constitutional powers he can utilise over his Cabinet, and Parliament as a whole.

But, these relationships can all come undone if he does not use these powers wisely. As some PMs have found to their cost! Gordon Brown, like Margaret Thatcher before him, ruled through imposing their personality. But this approach breeds resentment. The Prime Minister should be in control. He picks the team and can re-shuffle at will. But style matters.

The PM has control over the Cabinet agenda; what can be discussed, for how long and also what will not be discussed at all. Tony Blair was clearly in control of the Cabinet. Meetings famously lasted no more than half an hour.

His style of leadership was often described as "sofa government". He preferred to make decisions outside of the Cabinet, with his trusted special advisers, than with his Cabinet colleagues.

Do PMs just appoint their allies into the Cabinet to keep control?

Yes and No.

Tony Blair, like Margaret Thatcher, had a political vision of how he wanted to govern and where he wanted to take the country. Blair sought to "modernise" the UK. He therefore appointed like-minded "modernisers" who supported "the project". Most PMs will promote their most trusted allies into the Cabinet.

But, then, they will also promote their strongest rivals too. Gordon Brown is a classic example. Like Tony Blair, Gordon Brown was a New Labour supporter. But Gordon Brown held ambitions to be PM himself. He had, so the story goes, done a deal with Tony Blair that, Blair would stand down as PM after one term, allowing him to become PM. It never happened. Blair stayed on as PM for almost three full terms, winning three General Elections.

Instead of freezing Gordon Brown out of the Cabinet, and potentially creating a powerful focus for rebellion, Blair appointed Brown as Chancellor for ten years. He muzzled him through the doctrine of "collective responsibility".

David Cameron will have to compromise more than any other recent Prime Minister. He has two sets of rival politicians to keep on board, not just one.

What does collective responsibility mean?

Collective responsibility is the glue that holds the cabinet together. A Minister who will not publicly support the agreed Cabinet decision e.g. on tuition fees or on economy, has to resign. Brown never resigned during the Blair years. He disagreed over many issues. But he kept his silence. As PM, Brown was dogged by Cabinet resignations and couldn't control the Cabinet the way Tony Blair did.

Who all resigned?

The resignations of the WAGs (Women Against Gordon) in June 2009 was a central part of the "coup that never was". Caroline Flint and Hazel Blears resigned at the time of Labour's disastrous showing at the European Parliament elections.

Each had their different reasons for resigning but both were

"Blairites", rather than long term allies of the PM. James Purnell also resigned, telling the PM to quit, in order to save the Labour Party from defeat at the next General Election. He didn't. If more influential Cabinet ministers, such as Harriet Harman, Ed Balls or one of the Miliband brothers had quit, the PM's position would have been impossible.

What about controlling MPs?

Most MPs seek promotion. The PM can use this ambition to promote loyalty towards himself and the Cabinet. The parties all adopt a whip system for making sure MPs support party policy. MPs who rebel against the whip's advice are unlikely to be promoted.

Whips will try and persuade back benchers to support the Government. Rebellion against a 3-line whip is normally unforgiveable!

So, are MPs then just "lobby fodder"?

No. MPs can have a big influence on the Executive. When, in 2005, PM Tony Blair's Commons majority was cut from 162 to 66, the balance of power shifted away from the PM towards parliament. The Executive was defeated, for the first time, over plans to introduce 90 day detention for terrorist suspects.

In April 2009, Gordon Brown's plans to limit the number of Gurkhas who can settle in Britain was defeated in Parliament. Following a heated debate, MPs voted by 267 to 246 to defeat the Government's plans.

Government whips usually ensure that the Executive usually wins Parliamentary votes. The larger the Government majority, the less power back benchers have. But, a Government with a small majority and low opinion poll ratings will encourage back bench revolt.

David Cameron does not have a parliamentary majority and is reliant on Liberal Democrat whips as well as his own Conservative ones, to maintain parliamentary support for his Executive.

What about Prime Minister's Question Time?

PMQT is essentially theatrical. It doesn't change policy, but it can improve or damage party morale.

A PM or Opposition leader who is in command at PMQT can raise the spirits of MPs and party supporters, motivating them to campaign better in the country at large. However, a weakened PM will find PMQT an uncomfortable experience.

As Opposition leader David Cameron "scored points" in his debates with Gordon Brown in a way his predecessors never did with Tony Blair. Question Time became something of an ordeal for Gordon Brown.

Are there any other parliamentary opportunities for MPs to influence decision making?

Constructive debate and opposition normally takes place in the various parliamentary committees.

Some examples are: the Constitutional Affairs Committee, the Committee of Public Accounts or the Liaison Committee. MPs from different political parties often work together to amend policy in the light of evidence or strength of argument.

The House of Lords has the power to delay and possibly block Government legislation. The recent Labour Government was defeated in the Lords on a variety of issues such as anti-terrorism, fox hunting, sex education and ID cards.

Surely this is completely undemocratic, the House of Lords is completely unelected?!

You may well say so! The House of Lords is completely unelected.

Many peers inherited their seats from their fathers. Others are appointed by the Prime Minister, or are there through the church, or as law lords.

So, why do we still have a House of Lords who can stop laws made by the Government which was elected by the people?

Supporters of the Lords argue that it acts as a check on the power of the Executive. For example, how many students who protested over the raising of tuition fees (Deputy PM Nick Clegg pledged in the 2010 General Election campaign to abolish tuition fees) would complain if the Lords blocked this policy?

It is claimed that the Lords acts as a check on an imperfect voting system. Our famous First past the Post electoral system has often returned Government with huge parliamentary majorities but little support in the country. In 2005, Labour was famously elected as Government for five years with less than 36% of the total vote across the country.

It is also alleged that the Lords is less partisan and tribal than the Commons. It moreover, has time to scrutinise legislation, in a way the Commons does not.

But critics of the Lords argue that the hereditary principle is undemocratic. The system of appointees leads to "cronyism" and "jobs for the boys".

There have been numerous attempts to reform the Lords. As part of the Coalition Government's wider attempts to reform politics in the UK, a committee will be appointed which will bring forward proposals for a wholly or mainly elected House of Lords.

Are there likely to be any other reforms in the structure of decision making?

David Cameron has already reduced the number of Special Advisers.

Chairs and members of select committees are now to be elected by committee members, rather than being appointed by the whips.

There will be a new Backbench Business Committee, which will enable backbench MPs to decide how to use the time available to them.

And, there will be a referendum on the Alternative Voting System on 5 May 2011.

What other powers does the PM have?

The PM can appoint many others outside of the Cabinet e.g. senior civil servants, judges and heads of government bodies.

The PM can also appoint members of the House of Lords. Tony Blair, famously, was accused of giving peerages in return for donations to the Labour Party.

The PM can dominate the news agenda by going on the international stage. For example, by hosting meetings at Number 10 or going to NATO/UN summits. This can make an Opposition leader appear less important.

The PM has, or should have, control over the media agenda.

Anything he does or says is news and will be reported by the media. But, media is a double edged sword.

When the PM is in control, the media will be on his side. But it can put the PM on the defensive too. The *Daily Telegraph* and the *Daily Mail* are long-time Conservative supporters and campaigned against Gordon Brown from day one. But even *The Guardian* called on Gordon Brown to resign as PM. *The Sun* and other News International titles switched to the Conservatives for the 2010 General Election.

While the PM is not directly elected the way a US President is, and does not have the powers of a US President, the modern media increasingly personalise politics.

The personality of the PM is exposed 24/7, especially at election time. The success of a Government can depend on the public image of the PM.

David Cameron has brought in former News of the World editor, Andy Coulson, as his SPAD. Coulson's annual salary of £140,000 is higher than Deputy PM Nick Clegg's! This perhaps tells you something about modern politics!

Are there any other issues to consider?

Above all, a PM's authority will rest on his ability to make good decisions in response to the many unforeseeable social/economic and political events which will come his way.

Former Prime Minister Harold Macmillan was asked by a young journalist what can most easily steer a government off course. He replied "Events, dear boy. Events".

Gordon Brown dithered in October 2007 in the election that never was. He never really recovered.

It is early days for the new Coalition cabinet. As PM, David Cameron has to keep not just the Conservatives on side, but the Liberal Democrats too.

The "command and control" style of Gordon Brown cannot work for David Cameron. He must cajole and persuade Cabinet Ministers on a wide range of issues to support him.

The Conservatives had been out of power for 13 years. They are desperate for the Coalition to work. This explains why Vince Cable was not sacked from the Cabinet for his outspoken views on Cabinet relations and BSkyB.

Can senior Civil Servants have an influence on decision-making?

Most people's view of civil servants is coloured by the wonderful BBC series "Yes Minister".

The theme of the series is the way in which devious Civil Servants manipulate Government Ministers. Ministers are, after all, here today, gone tomorrow. Civil Servants, on the other hand, work in Government departments much longer.

In reality, the relationship between civil servant and Minister is symbiotic; each depends on the other. What is good for the civil servant is good for the Minister and vice versa. What is it senior Civil Servants do?

The Civil Service Code outlines the values civil servants are expected to uphold in all their dealings with Government and the public;

Integrity

Honesty

Impartiality

Objectivity

The job of the civil servant is to offer advice in an impartial, objective way, no matter the individual civil servant's political viewpoint. For example, in May 2010, after the Coalition Government was formed, the civil service had to stop supporting a Labour government and start supporting a Conservative/Liberal Democrat Government.

The civil service will brief the Prime Minister on the questions the Leader of the Opposition is likely to ask. The PM will have an army of civil servants providing him with arguments and statistics at his fingertips.

The civil service has been criticised for recruiting too many of its "fast track" graduates from Oxford and Cambridge universities. The Left sees the civil service as too establishment minded. The Right sees the civil service as too biased in favour of the public sector.

What about SPADs?

Special advisers ("SPADs") are defined as "temporary civil servants", who are exempt from the traditional requirement of officials that they should behave impartially and with objectivity, freeing them to brief politically for ministers.

Tony Blair famously confided in SPADs, such as Jonathan Powell, more than Cabinet colleagues. He was always at Tony Blair's side, just below the radar. Blair made decisions outside of Cabinet in bilateral meetings with his Special Advisers. This approach was termed "sofa government".

What influence, if any, do pressure groups have?
There are an increasing number of sophisticated pressure groups in the UK who aim to influence political decision making.

Thanks to developments such as Freedom of Information laws, the litigation culture, the internet, social networking and a 24/7 media, pressure groups are aware of their power. They are becoming increasingly strategic and professional in their operations.

Are there any examples of pressure groups having success?
After years of campaigning for the abolition of hunting with dogs, the League against Cruel Sports (LASC) must have been delighted when the Hunting Act, which outlawed the practice, was passed in 2005.

But, if anything, the League's campaigning has increased. LASC is being pro-active, rather than re-active. It is building public support in case the new Coalition Government decides on a new Hunting Law.

Its blood spattered website and emotive video seeks to win the hearts and minds of the public. "Keep Cruelty History" is using both new and old methods of campaigning to keep public opinion on its side.

Why do some pressure groups succeed?
The smaller a Government party's majority is in the House of Commons, the greater chance there is that pressure groups can have an influence.

Likewise, a Government with poor opinion poll ratings and backbenchers with fragile minorities will be more vulnerable to pressure group campaigns.

Pressure groups themselves need to be focused and strategic. The 2009 Gurkha campaign was a textbook case of effective pressure group campaigning;

It had a popular cause. The Nepalese Gurkhas have fought on Britain's side in many conflicts for over 200 years. Yet, the Labour Government refused to let retired Gurkha servicemen live in the UK. The campaign, led by actress Joanna Lumley, whose father served with the 6th Gurkha Rifles, won all retired Gurkhas the right to live in the UK.

Joanna Lumley was a media savvy and articulate figurehead. She exploited the weaknesses of an unpopular Government and a divided Cabinet. Famously, she ran rings round the hapless and hopeless Government Minister, Phil Woolas, live on TV news.

What methods do pressure groups use?

Sometimes, especially for outsider groups, a mass demonstration is important. The aim is obviously to change government policy but given that this may be unlikely, the purpose of a mass demonstration may be to boost the morale of pressure group members as well as gain media attention.

Stop the War Coalition admit its demonstrations didn't stop the invasion of Iraq, but it may have had more long term success in putting pressure on Government to be more accountable e.g. forcing inquiries into the war and also perhaps in making future invasions less likely. Likewise, the student demonstrations against the raising of tuition fees may not have succeeded in the short term but they may have a more long term effect in preventing the Government from making other cuts in student incomes.

Increasingly, pressure groups are using social networking sites to build support for their cause. For example, the anti-Fascist "Hope Not Hate" uses Facebook to organise its anti BNP activities.

Are some groups more influential than others?

Outsider groups are those whose aims do not enjoy the support of the Government. They tend to adopt media based, high profile stunts to capture public attention. Stop the War coalition would be a good example of an outsider pressure group.

Governments do not wish to be seen to back down to the demands of outsider groups.

By contrast, insider groups have the support and attention of Government. Government will often approach them for advice. They will often have long standing and regular discussions with Government. Some groups can go both inside and out, depending on the ideology of the Government of the day. The Confederation of British Industry (CBI) is a good example of an insider pressure group.

Trade unions were more "inside" under the Labour Governments but are likely to have less influence under the Conservative/Lib Dem coalition. Likewise, while New Labour was very pro-business, business groups will feel more "in the loop" with a Conservative Prime Minister.

Can the media have an influence over decision making?

Without a doubt.

The television media has a legal obligation to be politically neutral. But, the print media can be as biased as it likes.

No-one knows for sure whether Britain's most read newspapers can decide a General Election. But, no contender for power wants to take any chances. Owners of the big newspapers can, therefore, exercise power over Downing Street on the basis that "we'll support you, if you'll support us"

For example, the UK's tabloid newspapers are obsessed with immigration! Perhaps readers do not share their newspaper's views on immigration, but it would be a bold Government that was prepared to challenge *The Daily Express*, *The Mail*, *The Star* and *The Sun*. New Labour always fretted over what "middle England" thought. Has immigration policy been decided by the tabloid media?

In 2009, the Daily Telegraph's campaign which revealed MPs' expense claims led to public outrage, forcing Gordon Brown and his Cabinet to hastily change the laws on what MPs could legitimately claim.

One of Tony Blair's first acts upon becoming Labour leader was to win the support of Rupert Murdoch, owner of News International. *The Sun, The Times, The News of the World, The*

Sunday Times and *BSkyB* are just part of Rupert Murdoch's media empire. *The Sun* backed Blair at every General Election he fought as Labour leader. He won all three.

Tony Blair spoke to Rupert Murdoch three times in nine days in the run-up to the invasion of Iraq. Murdoch is also said to have been very influential on the Blair Government's policies on Europe and immigration.

With *The Sun* and *The Times* in the bag, Tony Blair and his Director of Communications, Alastair Campbell made sure that the Government's version of events made the right kind of news in the other media outlets.

Study Theme 1D Electoral Systems, Voting and Political Attitudes

> ➤ Good and bad points about The First Past the Post, Additional Member System and Single Transferable Vote
> ➤ Voting patterns; explanations of voting behaviour.
> ➤ The shaping of political attitudes through the media; opinion polls; referenda; voter participation.

What are the voting systems we have in the UK?

There are FOUR voting systems in use in the UK at the moment.

First Past The Post (FPTP) is used for UK General Elections.

Additional Member System (AMS) is used for Scottish parliament elections.

Single Transferable Vote (STV) is used for Scottish Local authority elections.

Party List system used for European parliament elections.

Why can't we just have one voting system?

A very good question!

Party politics, not democracy, explains why we have each of our systems.

Labour and Conservative parties both prefer FPTP because they have more chance of winning under FPTP. Their voters are concentrated in constituencies which are based on social class.

The Liberal Democrats and SNP favour STV, as their votes are dispersed across wider areas.

AMS is a compromise between the majoritarian FPTP and the

proportional system of STV. It has a proportional element but it is not, strictly speaking, a proportional system, as the majority of MSPs are elected by its FPTP element.

The Party List system, used for European elections, is not favoured by any of the UK's major parties.

In May 2011 there will be a referendum to introduce a fifth electoral system; the Alternative Vote Plus (AV+). No one party actually prefers this system. The Liberal Democrats would prefer STV and the Conservatives FPTP. But, the Coalition Government has compromised in proposing the AV+, which is slightly more proportional than FPTP.

What happens in UK FPTP elections?

649 "mini" elections take place, one in each constituency, or "seat". The party that wins the most seats wins the election.

What are its good points?

FPTP usually produces a decisive result which gives a Government a clear majority to deliver its election promises over a five year period. This happened with Tony Blair's clear victories in 1997, 2001 and 2005.

FPTP also enables by-elections to occur during the term of a Parliament. This allows voters to express their dissatisfaction with the Government of the day, if they choose. For example, Glasgow East in 2008, which returned an SNP MP, and Norwich in 2009 which returned a Conservative MP.

A third advantage is that voters have just the one representative who is responsible for their constituency. This, it is claimed, improves accountability.

What about its bad points?

FPTP doesn't always deliver a decisive result. FPTP can create coalition governments as well, for example, the current UK Conservative/Liberal Democrat Coalition. Did anyone vote for a coalition?

Is FPTP democratic? In 2005, Labour achieved just 36% of the popular vote yet governed the country for five years. Is this fair?

FPTP does, usually, create strong government. But is strong government good government? For example, would we have had Poll Tax or the Iraq war if Labour had to share power?

FPTP may foster voter apathy. FPTP has created many safe seats for Labour and Conservative parties. It is estimated that 382 out for the 649 Commons seats are "safe". Why bother voting if you live in one of these seats?

What about the AMS?

AMS is used for Scottish Parliament elections. It is a hybrid of FPTP and PR systems.

The Scottish Parliament has129 MSPs; 73 constituency MSPs and 56 Regional "List" MSPs. Voters vote twice: the first vote elects a constituency MSP, the second vote elects Regional List MSPs.

What are its good points?

AMS gives smaller parties a chance of representation. If 5% of voters vote Green, why should the Greens not have 5% of the representation?

Given Scottish voting patterns it is unlikely that any one party will have complete control over Parliament. Which should, in theory, mean that politicians are required to talk to each other and listen and compromise in a grown up way.

In 1999 and 2003 Scottish Parliament elections, Labour won the most seats, but did not have an overall majority. Labour and the Liberal Democrats entered into a coalition to run Scotland.

In 2007, the SNP won the most seats and again did not have an overall majority. It could not agree on terms for a coalition with the Liberal Democrats and has governed as a minority government on an issue by issue basis.

The AMS does not guarantee that one party will dominate, but given Scottish voting behaviour, it makes one party domination highly unlikely.

AMS should, in theory, encourage people in all parts of the country to vote. Every vote counts. Even in "safe" seats, there is an incentive to vote.

What are its bad points?

AMS produces "unelected" MSPs. For example, the SNP's List MSP Stefan Tymkewycz resigned just a few weeks after becoming an MSP. There was no by-election. Instead the SNP could choose any party member to replace him as an MSP. It chose Shirley-Anne Sommerville. Does this make the party machine more powerful than voters?

AMS produces MSP turf wars. Do List MSPs tread on the turf of constituency MSPs, who may think of themselves as the real MSP?

What about STV?

STV was introduced in Scotland in 2007 for the local authority elections. There will be another round of STV elections in 2012.

STV has multi member constituencies.

What are its good points?

Voting is easy. Voters rank candidates 1, 2, 3 etc in order of preference. They can vote for different members of the same party or vote for different parties. It is up to the voter

All votes count. STV voting is highly proportional. So voters should get what they voted for.

STV ends "safe seats", giving new or previously disadvantaged parties a greater chance.

STV empowers voters, not political parties. Voters have multiple choices, not just one vote.

STV means that deadbeat politicians can be rejected by the voters. No politician can take their seat for granted. In these days of expense scandals and low public esteem for politicians, representatives need to be more accountable.

What are its bad points?

It is harder for smaller parties to be elected than with the AMS. The "threshold" to be elected is higher.

Multi members could, in theory, confuse voters. Who does a voter go to?

If he/she goes to one Councillor, will the others be offended?

STV often leads to coalition government. This, in theory, could create unrepresentative and potentially unpleasant "kingmakers".

What conclusions can we come to about voting systems?
The issues are complex.

There is no one perfect system.

All voting systems have their strengths and weaknesses.

What are the main influences on how we vote?
There are many influences on voters in the UK. They are complex. They are changing. They are also inter-related, not separate.

We all have a social class. We all have a gender. We all have a race.

The media is also an influence. But there are many different types of media. And the different social classes access different kinds of media.

Is social class still a big influence?
Yes.

Social class remains a key influence. But, it's not what it was.

Up until the 1970s there was a clear two party system, with Labour perceived to be championing the working class, the Conservatives the middle and upper classes.

Since then, the middle class has grown in size. All the major parties now compete for the middle ground.

The FPTP system also encourages parties to ignore "safe" seats and win over floating voters in marginal constituencies. The Electoral Reform Society claims that 382 out of the 649 seats are so safe that any opposition vote is a wasted vote.

It is the party which wins the most seats throughout the country who wins UK General Elections. Not the party which wins the most votes.

But to win seats, you need to win votes.

There are 649 seats in total and each is a distinct geographical area. These areas are separated by social class. Richer people tend to live next to other richer people. Poorer people can only afford to live next to other poorer people.

So, many seats are either "safe" Conservative or "safe" Labour, depending on their social class composition. Labour continues to do best among poorer sections of the community. Voters tend to vote for the party which they feel represents their economic interest. The sociologist Danny Dorling points out that it was voters in the wealthiest constituencies which swung most firmly towards David Cameron.

Does nationality make a difference?
It seems to. But, it's a North/South divide as much as a Scottish/English divide.

Labour is strongest in the Northern cities of the UK and the Conservatives in the South.

In 2010, Scottish voters, perhaps seeing the General Election as a two horse race between Labour and Conservatives, returned Labour MPs with increased majorities. Labour won in even the most affluent areas, e.g. East Renfrewshire.

The Conservatives won just one seat in the whole of Scotland.

What about gender?
Women used to have a strong attachment to the Conservatives.

In fact, if it wasn't for the female vote, Labour probably would have won every post-war General Election up until 1979. Since then, their vote has been up for grabs. Gender is linked to social class. Poor women, like poor men, tend to vote Labour. *Middle class* women are more likely to be floating voters.

You mean "school gate mum?"
Yes.

School Gate Mum is the British version of the "Soccer Mums" found in the USA. They are working women who have demanding lives, balancing work and family responsibilities.

The Conservatives won clear majorities among women who have a career or have greater disposable income. A vital demographic group. Part of the Cameron agenda was for the Conservatives to have more female candidates and be more family friendly.

What about younger voters?
Traditionally younger voters are more likely to support parties promising social change.

For some time, the Conservatives' core vote has been among

older, affluent voters. But, in 2010, the Conservatives promoted a more youthful identity. The Conservatives this time did much better among younger voters....while keeping its core elderly vote.

Race?

Black voters, traditionally, are more likely to be Labour supporters. So too are Asian voters, but not as strongly as blacks. Labour, in general, has been seen to be more sympathetic to the needs of minority ethnic voters.

But, David Cameron worked hard to lose the Conservatives image of the "nasty party". The Conservatives made big efforts to win the votes of minority voters.

Gordon Brown's slogan "British jobs for British workers" was, ironically, taken up by the BNP. The BNP, with its explicitly racist message, failed to win any seats.

What effect does the media have?

Newspapers, especially tabloids, attempt to influence the result of elections. But there are other forms of media: television and new media such as websites, blogs and social media.

It is important to:
Firstly, discriminate between the different forms of media.
Secondly, consider the ways the various media try to influence.
Thirdly, assess the parties' competence in using the media.
Lastly, evaluate the impact of the media.

What forms of media are there?

These days, voters are exposed a diverse range of media.

In 2010, the first ever UK leaders' debates took place, with three debates on ITV, Sky and BBC. Around 10 million people watched the first debate on ITV.

Nick Clegg performed very well and the rise in support for the Liberal Democrats in the polls led many to believe the leaders' debates would have a decisive influence. But, the Liberal Democrats vote increased by a mere 1%.

Perhaps this is because, unlike in the USA, we do not vote directly for our political leader. It may also have been a reflection on the

FPTP voting system, where a vote for the Liberal Democrats was, all too often, in reality a "wasted vote".

Barack Obama's success in the USA was, in part, attributable to his skilful use of the new media. So, the political parties took social networking and Web 2.0 media very seriously in 2010. All the parties' websites had interactive features. They also used social network sites such as Youtube, Twitter and Facebook. This is all very clever, if, and only if, they are used well....

But, in 2010 the Old Media dominated. The first TV debate was watched by 9.4 million people. *The Sun* is read by 8 million people every day. By contrast, 79% of Britons could not re-call any online electioneering, not even an email.

How does the media try to influence voters?

Television media has to comply to strict rules over bias. But newspapers, especially tabloids can be very biased.

After much deliberation, in September 2009, just as Gordon Brown was about to deliver his Leaders' speech to the Labour Party conference, Rupert Murdoch's Sun newspaper picked its moment and declared its support for the Conservatives.

The newspaper, like the *Daily Express* and the *Daily Mail*, ran imbalanced and partisan articles on why Labour shouldn't be re-elected.

Does the support of *The Sun* decide elections?

Not on its own, obviously. But its support can't do any harm. It is the nations most read newspaper.

The Sun traditionally backs the winner, but then again, it usually waits to see who is most likely to win before it decides who to back.

Between 2005 and the time *The Sun* formally endorsed David Cameron in September 2009, Sun readers had already swung to the Conservatives by 12.5%. In other words, they'd decided to vote Tory before The Sun asked them to.

But then during the election itself, between the 6th of April when the Prime Minister called the election and election day, Sun readers swung back to the Tories.

Given the closeness of the 2010 General Election result, perhaps, this time, it was The Sun wot won it?

On the other hand, in the 2007 Scottish Parliament elections, all of the tabloid press attacked the SNP.

But the SNP won the election and also became the largest party in Scottish local government. We know the tabloid media try and have an influence. But, we should not assume it is a decisive influence. Many other factors come into play.

What about the parties' own campaigns?

In these days of celebrity, the image of the leader takes on more and more importance. While a party's campaign will not, on its own, win an election, a badly organised campaign can certainly lose one.

Parties require a good "air" attack via the media, but also a good "ground war"; phone calls, emails, leaflets and enthusiastic campaigners in communities. Labour was attacked by The Sun and put on the defensive.

But, it didn't help itself by scoring spectacular "own goals", such as Gordon Brown's infamous criticisms of, and subsequent apology, to "that bigoted little woman" filmed live by Sky News. The episode was further evidence, if it was required, that the PM was out of touch with ordinary voters.

SOCIAL ISSUES IN THE UK

Study Theme 2
Wealth and Health Inequalities

Need to Know

➤ Evidence of inequalities in wealth and health
➤ Causes of inequalities in wealth and health
➤ Consequences of inequalities in wealth and health.
➤ The extent of social and economic inequalities relating to gender and race
➤ Government responses to deal with gender and race inequalities
➤ The principles of the Welfare State
➤ The debate over individual and collective responsibility for health and welfare

What evidence is there of inequalities in wealth and health?

Loads. First of all, the UK is becoming a more unequal society.

While incomes and living standards for all Britons have grown in recent years, inequality between the classes has grown too. The top 10% of individuals in the UK now receive 40% of all personal income. The top 0.1% get 4.3% of all income – the highest figure in the UK since the 1930s, and three times as much as they received as a share of income in 1979.

The Joseph Rowntree Foundation (JRF) estimates that child poverty will fall from 2.9 million to 2.3 million by 2010 – 600,000 short of the Government's target.

To meet its target for 2010, according to the JRF, the Government would have to invest an estimated £4.2 billion a year in benefits and tax credits above its present plans. The allocation of an additional £2 billion since 2006 has been offset by an unexpected rise in child poverty between 2004 and 2007 and the increased costs of the recession.

Overall, in 2009, there were 11 million people living in relative poverty in the UK, a figure that has gone up by 300,000 since 2006. By 2020, without new policies to help low-income families, child poverty is projected to rise to 3.1 million.

Ok, I see the big picture, what about some stats on inequalities?

In Scotland in 2006, healthy life expectancy at birth was 67.9 years for men and 69 years for women. In the most deprived 15% of areas in Scotland in 2005-06, healthy life expectancy at birth was considerably lower, at 57.3 years for men and 59 years for women.

The rate of pregnancy among 13- to 15-year-old girls in the most deprived fifth of areas is twice as high as the average, and four times as high as in the least deprived fifth.

A higher proportion of babies born to mothers living in the most deprived fifth of the population have a low birth weight than those born to mothers living in the most affluent areas (9% compared to 5% in 2004-05).

Almost four-fifths of 5 year olds in the most deprived areas have some decayed teeth compared to two-fifths of those in the least deprived areas.

In Scotland in 2006, people on a low household income, or reported finding it difficult to manage on their household income, had poorer mental wellbeing than those with a high household income or who reported finding it easy to manage on their income.

Those living in the most deprived 10% of areas of Scotland have a suicide risk double that of the Scottish average.

Is it to do with unhealthy lifestyles?

Unhealthy lifestyles don't help, that's for sure. There are clear class inequalities in unhealthy living.

In Scotland in 2006, more than two thirds of the total alcohol-related deaths were in the most deprived two fifths of areas.

49% of men in the most deprived areas smoke regularly,

compared to 26% of men in the least deprived areas. The divide is similar for women: 43% smoke in the most deprived areas, compared to 24% in the least deprived.

Drug-related deaths have increased by 95 per cent since 1997 in Greater Glasgow and Clyde NHS Trust. In 2006, 43% of the total number of methadone users in Scotland were in Greater Glasgow.

It is estimated that in Glasgow more than 6,000 children are living with a parent who has a substance abuse problem.

The five authorities with the highest premature death rates are Glasgow City, West Dunbartonshire, Inverclyde, Dundee and North Lanarkshire. These are all authorities with serious problems of social deprivation.

"Scotland" is not the sick man of Europe. If we were to take these authorities, i.e. the poorest ones, out of the equation, Scotland would be one of the healthiest countries in the world! There are plenty of areas in Scotland where people have a very high standard of living, including, believe it or not, parts of Glasgow!

So, if we could get the poor to start living a bit more sensibly we'd tackle health inequalities?

Yes and No. Better diet, more exercise and less cigarettes, alcohol and drugs would undoubtedly help. But, the middle classes drink and smoke too!

So, why aren't health statistics as bad for the better off?

A very good question. So, let's consider the views of Dr Harry Burns.

Who's he?

Dr Harry Burns is the Chief Medical Officer for Scotland. He has spent a large part of his professional career researching the relationship between poverty and ill health. His conclusions are that there are clear links between poverty and health inequality. They are partly to do with lifestyles. A bad diet does lead to higher levels of cholesterol.

But his research shows that there is a "biology of poverty".

While the middle classes may have unhealthy lifestyles, they are better able to cope with illnesses. From a very early age, a settled and less stressful childhood appears to strengthen the body's immune system. By contrast, a chaotic, stressful childhood weakens the body's immune system and ability to combat illness.

This is why Burns has advised the Scottish Government to prioritise preventative healthcare, focusing on identifying and intervening in the lives of at risk children in the early years of their lives.

Ok, so much for class inequality, what evidence is there of racial inequality?

Ethnic minorities in the UK can expect to encounter various forms of racism.

Racism is not necessarily based on colour.

Racism can be directed against people of the same colour, but based on their nationality. So, there can be anti-Irish, anti-English or anti-Polish racism by people of the same skin colour. And, of course, white Scots may, on occasion, be the victims of racism.

Overt racism can take the form of name calling, direct discrimination, assault and general harassment. It can be seen and identified. Islamophobia is one form of overt racism which has been on the increase.

Institutional racism is more subtle. This is where the attitudes and practices of an organisation are racist and prejudiced against particular groups. The term came into the public domain after the botched investigation by the Metropolitan Police into the murder of Stephen Lawrence in 1993. The force accepted it was institutionally racist.

Many of Scotland's minority ethnic community workers are employed in low level, poorly paid jobs. Retail and catering are two of the main sectors, often through self employment (newsagent or grocery store), or being employed by other minority ethnic employers, e.g. working in restaurants.

Some people speak, not of a glass ceiling (gender discrimination), but a "glass door" for minority ethnic men and women. If you don't see people like you in top level jobs, it may become a self-fulfilling prophecy.

There are also racial stereotypes, fuelled by Islamophobia, which make employers less likely to employ or promote minority ethnic candidates.

The 2009 Race for Opportunity Report showed that Black and Minority Ethnic (BME) workers make up 10.3% of the population but only 8.5% of the workforce and just 6.3% of those in management positions. A 2010 survey by the charity Business in the Community, "Aspiration and Frustration", found that despite years of Government legislation, equality of opportunity remained a long way off.

It concluded that some of the best-paid professions such as banking, law, politics and the media were not seen as a realistic option for BMEs. Those with an historic reputation for racism, such as the police and armed forces, are still seen as unwelcoming to minorities.

The 'caring' professions, education and medicine, which have a positive history of BME recruitment are seen as good options, but as less well-paid and offering less career progression, particularly education.

What has government done to create equal opportunities in race?

Overt racial discrimination (i.e. name calling, bullying, refusal of jobs) has been illegal since the Race Relations Act of 1976. This law makes it illegal to discriminate in jobs, housing and public services, on the basis of a person's ethnic background, although amazingly the police service was, at the time, omitted from this Act.

The Race Relations Act was incorporated into the new Equalities Act (October 2010)

The Scottish Government has also launched a variety of anti-racist campaigns and supported the "Show Racism the Red Card" initiative.

The Equality Act 2010 incorporates all previous Equalities legislation. Rights and Responsibilities have either:

Stayed the same. Direct discrimination still occurs when "someone is treated less favourably than another person because of a protected characteristic".

Changed – for example, employees are now be able to complain of harassment even if it is not directed at them, if they can demonstrate that it creates an offensive environment for them.

Been extended. Associative discrimination (direct discrimination against someone because they associate with another person who possesses a protected characteristic) will cover age, disability, gender reassignment and sex as well as race, religion and belief and sexual orientation.

Been introduced for the first time. The legislation enables employers to favour under-represented groups during the recruitment process – provided the candidates are of equal suitability – to increase the diversity of their workforces. This is comparable to the affirmative action programmes of the USA.

What evidence is there of gender inequality?

There is considerable evidence to show there are still considerable inequalities between the genders.

One of the reasons for gender inequality is the glass ceiling. A study in 2008 by the Royal Economic Society found that professional and managerial women who became mothers moved down the job ladder after returning from having a child. 2/3 took clerical or lower skilled jobs.

Women who managed shops, salons or restaurants were even more adversely affected. Almost 50% gave up their managerial responsibilities to become sales assistants, hairdressers or similar roles. Teaching and nursing were the best careers for moving to part-time hours, but even here 10% quit for lower skill jobs.

The New Earnings Survey of 1991-2001 highlighted the continued problem of the few number of jobs available on a part-time basis, but which offer pay and conditions comparable to full-time work. As it is more often women who do these jobs, this makes a major contribution to income inequality. 40% of women who work have part-time jobs, a number which includes the majority of mothers.

The glass ceiling can be subtle and perhaps unconscious. But, the Fawcett Society has found evidence of more direct discrimination against women, particularly in the financial sector.

Its "Sexism in the City" campaign highlights the fact that women are disadvantaged by outdated sexist job structures and attitudes. Women are excluded from power: only 11% of FTSE 100 company directors are women. Every year 30,000 women lose their jobs because they are pregnant. Two-thirds of low-paid workers are women. Women working full-time earn 17% less than men.

What has government done to create equal opportunities in gender?

The 2010 Equality Act updates the landmark gender laws, such as the Equal Pay Act and the Sex Discrimination Act.

It is still illegal to treat someone less favourably on the basis of their gender. For example, a claim for equal pay may be made by either a woman or a man claiming equal pay with one or more "comparators" of the other sex. "Dinner ladies", for example, do work of equal value as janitors, but, historically, the two jobs have been divided on gender grounds with one much better paid than the other.

Scottish local authorities have paid out millions to settle claims from female employees who have carried out work of equal value tomen, but did not receive equal pay.

The 2010 Equality Act extends the law in some new ways. It requires all public sector employers and larger companies to publish pay audits revealing the differences between male and female staff.

Pay secrecy clauses which prevent employees revealing their salaries are illegal.

Employers are now able to take "positive action" to recruit groups who are under-represented in their workforce, where they have a choice between two candidates who are equally suitable. The Equality and Human Rights Commission will publish guidance on the range of actions employers will be able to take.

What about social class? Is anything being done to create more equal opportunities?

For the first time, the 2010 Equality Act puts a new duty on Government departments, local authorities and NHS bodies to consider what action they can take to reduce so-called 'socio-economic' inequalities i.e. your family background or where you were born.

Education authorities, for example, now have a duty to encourage pupils from poorer backgrounds to apply to successful schools in their area. Health authorities are required to allocate funds towards those with worst health records. Development agencies need to encourage more successful bids for grants from those living in deprived areas.

In terms of health, the Scottish Government's Equally Well initiative has set up a Ministerial Taskforce on Health Inequalities. Dr Harry Burns, Scotland's Chief Medical Officer, has played a leading role in its approach. There is now a much greater focus on early intervention in children's lives.

This is why the Scottish Government has attempted, among other things, to introduce free school meals for all in P1-P3. In April 2008, the charge for a single prescription was reduced from £6.85 to £5.00. This has been reduced by a further £1 a year, until 2011, when prescription charges will be abolished altogether. Coincidentally, just in time for the Scottish Parliament elections!

The gaps in wealth and health in the UK are vast.

All UK political parties seek equality in health care. All are committed to the principles of the NHS. But health is very strongly related to wealth. All UK political parties are committed to *equality of opportunity* in wealth but not equality as such.

To create greater equality in wealth, re-distribution of wealth is required, not just wealth creation. This would mean controversial choices for example, reform of the tax and inheritance system and a re-drawing of school catchment areas. While the major political parties chase the "centre-ground", these reforms are unlikely.

What are the main principles of the welfare state?

The original ideals of the welfare state, as outlined in the post-war Beveridge report, were to provide a comprehensive system of social insurance 'from cradle to grave'.

It proposed that all working people should pay a weekly contribution to the state. In return, the state would pay benefits to the unemployed, the sick, the retired and the widowed.

Beveridge wanted to ensure that there was an acceptable minimum standard of living in Britain below which nobody fell.

Are these principles out of date?

No major political party is saying that these principles are out of date. But, they do say that we now live in a society which is very different from anything Beveridge could have imagined. New solutions are needed to these new social issues.

For example?

We all live longer for a start, meaning the Government has to fund pensions for considerably longer. As people get older, they are more likely to develop long-term costly illnesses such as dementia, which was rare in the 1940s.

We have many more lone parent families than we did in Beveridge's time. Beveridge did not envisage long term mass unemployment or people living on benefits for a long time. Neither did Beveridge foresee health issues such as drug dependency and obesity.

Modern governments have to find solutions to these new social issues.

Are modern day governments more individualist than collective?

The emphasis varies.

Margaret Thatcher identified the trade unions and organised labour as the barrier to her social revolution. Where Beveridge sought collective solutions, the Thatcher-led Conservatives sought individual solutions.

When Labour famously became "New Labour" in 1994, it abandoned traditional socialism. The "Third Way", whilst retaining "old Labour values", embraced these in "a modern setting", to take in ideas which were previously seen as "Tory".

Labour could now reach out to voters who supported working *with* the private sector rather than against it. These voters were pro-business and disliked "tax and spend" economics. This meant that Labour could keep its traditional voters (in England and Wales at least) and now pull in Conservative voters into the "big tent". New Labour believed in "welfare to work".

What is, or was, welfare to work?

Welfare to Work is an umbrella term for all the various initiatives the Labour Governments, both in Westminster and at Holyrood, have taken to move people from welfare to work.

New Labour believed that to tackle the five giant evils, people, if they are fit and able, need to be working. Therefore financial incentives were put in place to get people back to work, such as the National Minimum Wage and a variety of Tax Credits. The

Coalition Government has continued Labour's overall welfare to work approach but is being bolder in its attempts to get the long-term unemployed back to work.

What is the Coalition Government's big idea?The Conservatives have acknowledged that there is a link between poverty and bad health and/or poor education. The Conservatives speak of a "broken society".

David Cameron and his Work and Pensions Secretary, Iain Duncan Smith, seek to "heal" the so-called broken society by encouraging greater individual responsibility (a traditional Conservative approach) and use of the voluntary sector to help those prepared to face up to their problems.

The Government proposes the setting up of "vanguard communities". In these communities, individuals and voluntary groups will be funded to take over duties previously provided by the state.

These groups can run housing projects, schools, youth groups and cultural organisations. A "big society bank" will be established to finance charities and voluntary groups.

A new Welfare Reform Bill will also be passed which will make it tougher to claim out-of work benefits, especially Incapacity Benefit. Controversially, as part of its efficiency savings, Child Benefit will be abolished for those earning over £42,000.

Critics feel that the Conservatives' proposals are unrealistic and unworkable.

How, for example, do we actually get the long term unemployed, many of whom have serious mental health issues, back to work? Unemployment is rising and more job losses are on the way. Can the long-term unemployed really compete in the job market against skilled workers?

Critics say the Big Society is either nothing new – the Labour Governments worked with voluntary groups too – or that the Big Society is simply a smokescreen for big cuts in public services.

Others claim that only those with skills, time and contacts will be able to access the Big Society. The poor and the powerless will be left further behind, effectively ending the welfare state.

INTERNATIONAL ISSUES

Study Theme 3A The Republic of South Africa

Need to know

➤ How the South African political system works
➤ Trends in participation and representation in political life
➤ Differences and similarities between different political parties
➤ Social and economic inequalities among and within South Africa's racial groups
➤ Government social/economic strategies

Background

It is important to remember that democracy is very new to South Africa. Between 1848-1990, the country was governed by the racist apartheid system. Black South Africans were not citizens of their country and could not vote. They were forced to live in townships outside the big cities or, in the "bantustans" or "homelands", as the apartheid government referred to these areas.

Because of apartheid, South Africa was barred from the Olympic Games and all international sporting events. South African goods were boycotted and the African National Congress (ANC), led by its jailed leader, Nelson Mandela, waged an at times violent war against the apartheid state. Housing and schools in black areas were, and for the most part still are, inferior to white houses and schools because of apartheid.

As such, the political parties to some extent reflect the loyalties which developed during the struggles of apartheid. Most black voters retain their loyalty to the ANC which was the main driving force against apartheid.

The ANC Government still refers to the legacy of apartheid. This has left health, education and housing for the majority of South Africans in need of massive investment. The problems of crime can also be said to have some basis in the poverty and hopelessness of the apartheid years.

But, the ANC has been in power since 1994. Even many of its greatest supporters say progress is too slow and that apartheid cannot be blamed forever for the problems the nation faces. Some of these are self inflicted by poor leadership and badly thought out policies.

South Africa has three capital cities: Cape Town, the largest of the three, is the *legislative* capital; Pretoria is the *administrative* capital; and Bloemfontein is the *judicial* capital.

Its main racial groups are: Black African 79.5%, White 9.2%, Coloured 8.9% Indian or Asian 2.4%

There are great differences within black South Africans.

Major ethnic groups include the Zulu, Xhosa, Basotho (South Sotho), Bapedi (North Sotho), Venda, Tswana, Tsonga, Swazi and Ndebele, all of whom speak Bantu languages.

Crime is a major issue affecting all South Africans. Whites have most possessions to lose, but black on black crime in the townships is common. South Africa has more car-jackings, rapes and murders than almost any other country in the world.

There has been considerable "white flight" due to crime, but also due to poor public services. South Africa is one of the most unequal countries in the world. Low pay, unemployment, poor housing and HIV/AIDS all disproportionately affect poor black South Africans.

President Zuma came to power in May 2009. His supporters expect him to improve life for South Africa's poor.

While it is likely he will be more sympathetic towards the poor than his predecessor, Thabo Mbeki, Zuma's South Africa has continued to pursue a free market agenda, with the priority being to secure foreign investment.

The 2010 FIFA World Cup was a very, very big deal. South Africa was the first African nation to host a World Cup. Many doubted that South Africa, indeed any African nation, could host a successful World Cup.

They were wrong. 2010 was one of the most successful World Cups ever. Almost 3.2 million spectators poured into the 10 stadiums during the month long tournament. This gave South Africa 2010 the third highest attendance in the history of the World Cup, after the US-hosted tournament in 1994 and Germany's in 2006.

The South African Government is hoping for a legacy of increased foreign investment and tourism. We shall have to wait and see if the World Cup has delivered a long term legacy in improving social/economic life, or whether the costs totalling £2 billion could have been better spent elsewhere.

Does South Africa have a written constitution?

Yes. South Africa's political system is one of the most liberal and democratic in Africa.

The first item in the Preamble of the Constitution states that its aim is to "heal the divisions of the past and establish a society based on democratic values, social justice and fundamental human rights".

Just like the USA with its 50 states, South Africa has nine provinces; Eastern Cape, Gauteng, KwaZulu-Natal, Mpumalanga, Northern Cape, Limpopo, North West, Free State and Western Cape.

While the ANC dominates the parliament and political life, South Africa has a robust parliamentary opposition, most notably in the form of the Democratic Alliance (DA).

The country has a fully independent judiciary. In July 2010, Jackie Selebi, the country's top policeman, was found guilty of taking £1.2m rand (£103,000) in bribes.

There is a free and critical media, with newspapers such as the Mail & Guardian critical of the ANC.

Rights for minorities are included in the constitution. In 2006, same-sex marriages became legal in South Africa. It is the only African country to allow same-sex marriages.

What is the government structure?

South Africa is a federal state, consisting of a national government and nine provincial governments.

It has a bicameral parliament elected every five years, comprising of the 400-seat National Assembly and the 90-seat National Council of Provinces.

The role of local government in providing local democracy and public services is enshrined in the constitution. Unlike Scotland, public private partnerships are still being used to build new schools and hospitals.

General Elections are fought under a party list system of proportional representation. The last one was 2009. The next one will be 2014.

What happened at the 2009 General Election?

The ANC won overwhelming public support, again. But not the 2/3 majority to enable the party to change the country's constitution.

The ANC won control of 8 out of 9 provinces.

Zuma is a charismatic and personable President. He is popular with the poor and has overcome a great deal of personal problems. But, the white middle classes do not trust him. He has shown poor judgement in the past!

For example?

Having unprotected sex with a HIV+ ANC activist is pretty stupid. Especially if you are seeking to be President of a country where AIDS is a massive problem. Claiming that if you took a shower afterwards you might not get infected, hardly sends the right message either!

Zuma was also charged with rape for this incident but the charges were dropped. Likewise, corruption charges related to arms deals were also dropped against Zuma. Other incidents, such as the singing of the old ANC song, "Give me my machine gun", have not endeared him to the affluent whites he would like to remain living and working in South Africa.

In January 2010, it was revealed that Zuma, who had just married his third wife, was not only secretly engaged to a fourth woman, but that he had just fathered a child (perhaps his 20th) to another woman, the wife of one of his best friends!

Why did the ANC win?

Blacks make up almost 80% of South Africa. The ANC retains the loyalty of the vast bulk of black South Africans, so it was always going to be a case of how much the ANC won by, rather than whether it would win at all.

The creation of the Congress of the People (COPE) energised the ANC. The party could no longer take black votes for granted and it had to fight a real election campaign. The ANC spent around R200 million on the election, placing party president Jacob Zuma right at the centre. Zuma is popular with poor blacks, in a way the cold and managerial Thabo Mbeki never was.

By contrast, COPE's campaign was unprofessional and poorly-funded.

The ANC won just short of 2/3 of the votes, which would have enabled the party to change the South African constitution. However, Zuma will be pleased with the level of support the party received after another high turnout of voters (77%).

The Western Cape is now the only one of South Africa's nine provinces not governed by the ANC. The Democratic Alliance runs this province. But, the DA has not managed to overcome "racial politics" and is still seen by many of South Africa's poor as a "white party". The DA gained 16% of the national vote and 67 seats in the National Assembly.

The Zulu-based IFP won just 4.5% of the national vote. The ANC won the party's former stronghold of Kwazulu-Natal. The popularity of Zuma, a Zulu himself, impacted significantly on the IFP.

So, is the ANC an "elected dictatorship"?

It's a strange phrase this! Dictatorships tend not to have elections!

It's hardly the ANC's fault that 66% of South Africans choose to vote for the party. South African elections cannot be compared with the type of farce which takes place in neighbouring Zimbabwe.

While there may be isolated examples of bullying and intimidation, elections are free, fair and well supported.

That is not to say that the ANC has not been above criticism. As Lord Acton's famous phrase goes, "power tends to corrupt and absolute power corrupts absolutely".

Andrew Feinstein, a former ANC MP has told of how Thabo

Mbeki imposed AIDS denialism on government and stopped an investigation into a multi-billion-dollar arms deal.

Investigating the payment of up to $200 million worth of bribes, Feinstein alleges that there is a culture of corruption at the very highest levels of South African politics. The ANC's decision to abolish the elite crime-busting police unit, The Scorpions, alarmed many. The Scorpions were fearless investigators of corruption. Some believe that Zuma silenced them before they blew the whistle on ANC wrong-doing.

But there is still plenty of opposition to the ANC.

Trade Unions are still popular and powerful in South Africa. The Confederation of South African Trade Unions (COSATU) is at odds with the ANC and the government over several issues, most notably the way "black economic empowerment"—the policy of redistributing wealth into black hands—has enriched only a lucky, politically-connected few.

Is Zuma accumulating more power for himself?

Not necessarily. Zuma, as President, has extended power to his political opponents. As expected, some of his left wing supporters have been included in his Cabinet, but only in relatively, non-economic minor posts.

Trevor Manuel, one of Thabo Mbeki's conservative Ministers, left his post as Finance Minister. But he has been given a new position as the head of a national planning commission. He may become even more powerful than before. Manuel is widely seen as important for the ANC to ensure foreign investment.

Interestingly there was a place in the cabinet for the Afrikaaner based Freedom Front's (FF) Pieter Mulder, as deputy agriculture minister.

What are the main social/economic challenges facing the Zuma Government?

In no particular order, these are education, health, housing, poverty and crime. They are all connected.

Education is not just the key to a more highly skilled workforce, but a more informed and empowered population, able to make intelligent life choices.

The Zuma Government is spending 1/5th of its budget on education. The legacy of apartheid remains. Not just in shoddy school buildings and enormous class sizes. But in attitudes to education among teachers, most of whom are products of the apartheid years.

Housing. The number of people living in shantytowns has grown hugely in the past few years. Unlike townships such as Soweto, which were designated areas for blacks to live in under apartheid, the shantytowns are spontaneous settlements, set up by people fleeing the poverty and lack of opportunity in rural South Africa.

In the Foreman Road shanty town in Durban, residents say there are just five toilets between 7,000 of them, and only four water standpipes provided by the local council. There is no electricity, so the main hazard in Foreman Road is fire, caused by accidents with paraffin lamps. Residents suffer a lot of health problems, mainly stomach and respiratory ailments.

In Alexandra township people tell stories of huge rats that invade their shacks at night, as bold as wild dogs, biting sleeping children.

Health. Arguably President Mbeki's biggest failing was his inability to tackle the AIDS crisis. Mbeki first denied South Africa had an AIDS problem, then he appointed "Dr Garlic" as Health Minister who believed that AIDS could be treated by eating garlic and beetroot. AIDS drugs are now reaching sufferers, but many lives could have been saved by a proper strategy.

Poverty. The former homelands, for example, Limpopo, are the poorest parts of South Africa. South African unemployment, which stands officially at 26.7%, is in reality closer to 40%, one of the highest rates in the world. It is not uncommon for schools to have no electricity and class sizes of over 100. Children will often walk ten miles to school. Clean water is in short supply. Hospitals can be scary places.

Crime. Officially, there were 36,190 rapes in 2007-08 and 14, 201 car jackings but, of course, many crimes go unreported. About 50 people a day are murdered. The murder rate in the UK is 0.38 murders per day. The South African police have been unable to gain the arrests and convictions which could act as a deterrent. The carjackers, muggers and rapists simply believe that they will not get caught.

Any more statistics?

The percentage of people aged 15-49 living with HIV/AIDS: 18.1%. The UK figure is 0.11%. South Africa has 400 women per 100,000 who die giving birth. The UK's figure is 11 per 100,000. Average per capita income for South Africans is US$9,560. In the UK it's US$33,800. Average life expectancy in South Africa is 51 years. In the UK it's 79 years.

What is the Government doing about all of this?

After the overthrow of apartheid, the ANC felt it had to reassure the international financial community and the money markets that investments in South Africa were safe and that the government, with its trade union and SACP allies, was not going to nationalise everything in sight.

The ANC's main economic strategy, GEAR, sought to reassure international markets that widespread nationalisation and wealth redistribution were not on the agenda. GEAR sought to attract foreign investment, privatise industries and use public private partnerships to build hospitals, houses and schools.

The Accelerated and Shared Growth Initiative for South Africa (ASGISA) has replaced GEAR. This will involve spending 370 billion rand on public works, mainly infrastructure, to boost jobs and create more demand.

Black Economic Empowerment (BEE) is a form of affirmative action which aims to empower previously disadvantaged blacks giving them access to management positions and ownership of businesses. Organizations must comply with BEE regulations if they want to qualify for contracts from the government.

Bee has been pretty unpopular, hasn't it?

Not if you're one of the people who has benefitted from it!

The so-called "Black Diamonds" think BEE is great!

A report by the University of Cape Town's Unilever Institute said the number of "Black Diamonds" has grown by 30% in just over a year, to 2.6 million out of a total South African population of about 48 million.

The group is worth about R180 billion, representing 28% of the total South Africans spend.

Tokyo Sexwale, a former jailed ANC activist, is now a millionaire via his oil and diamonds investments.

So, inequalities in South Africa are not just between blacks and whites but between blacks themselves?

Absolutely.

South Africa has continued to be a very unequal country, one of the most unequal in the world.

To understand how many inhabitants of a country are poor, it is not enough to know a country's per capita income. The number of poor people in a country and the average quality of life depend on how equally or unequally income is distributed across the population. Brazil is normally cited as one of the most unequal countries in the world, but South Africa is now rivalling it.

In the past inequality in South Africa was largely defined along race lines. But, in recent years an emerging, and increasingly confident, black middle-class is fuelling a consumer boom while millions remain mired in unemployment and appalling living conditions.

There is now a sense of impatience over the pace of change in South Africa. For many, the country's advance towards Mr Mandela's vision of a "rainbow nation" has slowed to a crawl.

Was the 2010 World Cup a waste of precious resources?

Possibly.

The South African government spent £3 billion on the 2010 World Cup. It created an estimated 415,000 jobs, not all of them permanent ones.

The World Cup was an undoubted organisational triumph, partly because world expectations were unreasonably low. Many believed an African nation was incapable of staging a World Cup. There was a tremendous desire for the World Cup to succeed and widespread support within this sports-mad nation for the event to succeed.

Yet, there has been criticism.

£90m was invested in the world class health facilities demanded by FIFA. During the time of the World Cup, 17 infants died in public hospitals due to a lack of basic medical equipment. By 2015, the lives of almost 50,000 newborn babies and children could be saved if SA reached high and effective levels of prevention of mother-to- child transmission of HIV.

Study Theme 3B China

Need to know

➤ How the Chinese political system works
➤ The role of the Chinese Communist Party and the extent of political opposition.
➤ Issues over human rights
➤ Social and economic inequalities within China
➤ Government social/economic strategies

Background

A country which officially describes itself as "communist" has agricultural workers being paid 60p an hour. At the same time, China's rich pay the £190,000 annual subscription to play at the world's largest golf club – Mission Hills, in Hong Kong.

If there is a society in change in the Modern Studies syllabus this has to be the one. "Communist China" is experiencing an economic boom which has seen it become the world's 3rd largest economy. Especially since China joined the World Trade Organisation, an economic boom, described as the "economic miracle" has transformed the country, especially the interior. An awareness of the sheer scale and speed of such change is very important. The Chinese Communist Party is trying to modernise the country in a fraction of the time the UK and the USA had their industrial revolutions. This has an enormous impact on the poor, who are voiceless in this authoritarian political systeThe creation of the Three Gorges Dam is just one example of how human rights and environmental considerations have been an afterthought to the "economic miracle". The move from the countryside to the city has been described as the biggest population movement in human history.

The CCP while in charge of the media, a powerful army and a ruthless police cannot rule on brute force forever. No Government can. An army of desperate migrant workers will work for sweatshop wages now, but what if the economy hits recession (or even slower economic growth) and they lose what pitiful earnings they now have? The CCP must also make democratic concessions to the new, educated and worldly wise middle classes in its teeming cities. China is also struggling to control its millions of internet users, who continue to ask awkward questions about how the country is run.

These are fascinating times in China.

Does China have a written Constitution?

Yes. But it is one which grants the Chinese Communist Party (CCP) a special place.

Following from Karl Marx and Mao's idea of the "dictatorship of the proletariat", the CCP sees itself as "leading" China into communism.

In order to do this, "bourgeois" political parties are not allowed to win power and therefore deflect the party from its "historic" mission of leading the Chinese people to communism. The Chinese Constitution states that…

"The Communist Party of China is the vanguard both of the Chinese working class and of the Chinese people and the Chinese nation. It is the core of leadership for the cause of socialism with Chinese characteristics and represents the development trend of China's advanced productive forces, the orientation of China's advanced culture and the fundamental interests of the overwhelming majority of the Chinese people. The realization of communism is the highest ideal and ultimate goal of the Party……….

China is in the primary stage of socialism and will remain so for a long time to come. This is a historical stage which cannot be skipped in socialist modernization in China which is backward economically and culturally. It will last for over a hundred years"

The CCP has governed China since its victory over the Kuomintang (Chinese National Party) in 1949.

Despite the inequality, the poverty, the lack of human rights and democracy, the CCP claims that "Communism with Chinese Characteristics" is a society which is socialist and on the way to becoming fully communist. One day.

Does China not have a parliament, elected by the people?

The Chinese parliament, the 2,987 strong National People's Congress (NPC) meets in the capital, Beijing. Elections are held very four years. The next elections are in 2012. Only members of the Chinese Communist Party, its eight allied parties and sympathetic independent candidates are elected to the NPC. So, the NPC is, in reality, subordinate to the CCP.

China has 23 Provinces (if you include Taiwan, as the Chinese Government does): Anhui, Fujian, Gansu, Guangdong, Guizhou, Hainan, Hebei, Heilongjiang, Henan, Hubei, Hunan, Jiangsu, Jiangxi, Jilin, Liaoning, Qinghai, Shaanxi, Shandong, Shanxi, Sichuan, Taiwan, Yunnan and Zhejiang.

There are five "autonomous regions"; Guangxi, Nei Mongol, Ningxia, Xinjiang and Xiizang (Tibet).

The CCP is the largest political party in the world. It has 70 million members. Membership of the CCP is encouraged for students and intellectuals. Membership of the CCP has many advantages in securing jobs and good housing.

Hu Jintau is the CCP General Secretary and President of the People's Republic of China. Wen Jibao is the Premier (head of government).

Since 1979, it has been illegal to debate the relevance of the Four Principles of Chinese Communism:

- the principle of upholding the socialist path
- the principle of upholding the people's democratic dictatorship

- the principle of upholding the leadership of the Communist Party of China, and
- the principle of upholding Marxist-Leninist-Mao Zedong thought.

The media, including the internet, in China is strictly controlled by the CCP. Search engines and blogs which contain "subversive" phrases such as "democracy" or "freedom" are blocked. The CCP has even blocked access to Twitter.

Are there any opposition parties at all?
Eight minor opposition parties are allowed to participate in the political system.

But, they are not parties in the sense that we know them. They are not allowed to hold power in national elections. They do not even have a website where we can evaluate their policies! Some examples are the China Democratic National Construction Association, September 3 Society and the Chinese Peasants' and Workers' Democratic Party

The CCP allows the odd non-CCP politician to join the country's Cabinet, the Politburo. Chen Zhu, for example is the Health Minister, the first non CCP Minister for 40 years. But he has been tightly vetted by the CCP and he will be sacked if he deviates from the CCP line.

Does opposition to the CCP not take other forms?
Yes.

It is difficult to evaluate the depth of political opposition to the CCP because of the secrecy of the CCP's regime. But, there is a network of political activists who campaign for human rights. They attempt to hack through China's infamous internet bans and firewalls to discuss political reform.

What about Tibet?
There are nationalist groups based in Tibet and also Xinjiang "autonomous region" who campaign against what they see as China's occupation of their land.

Tibet made the news in 2008, as the Chinese authorities

suppressed protests for Tibetan independence. China "liberated" or, to be more accurate, invaded Tibet in 1950. Its leader, The Dalai Lama, has been in exile for the past 40 years. He lives in neighbouring India. He won the Nobel Peace Prize in 1989 for his advocacy of peaceful protest. His photograph is banned in China.

Hundreds of monks and nuns who have supported him are imprisoned by the Chinese government, in violation of fundamental human rights. Around 11% of the inmates of Tibet's notorious jails are imprisoned for publicly opposing the leadership of the CCP.

In July 2009, more than 200 people were killed and 1700 injured during inter-ethnic violence in Xinjian province between incoming Han Chinese and the native Uighurs. Some Uighurs would like independence from China and, like Tibetan nationalists, see the Han Chinese as an occupying force.

What happens to these activists if they are caught?

The CCP used the 9/11 attacks on the USA as an opportunity to crack down on its political opponents.

Hu Jintao's Zero Tolerance "strike hard" campaign has been popular for the way it has tackled crimes of burglary and violent assault, but peaceful political opponents have been its victims too.

Portrayed as "ethnic separatists, terrorists and religious extremists", dissenting voices have been imprisoned, placed under house arrest and harassed by the police. Since 1949, an estimated 50 million people have been taken to Laogai for "Re-Education Through Labour". They serve sentences of up to three years, entirely at the recommendation of the police, without having had a chance to defend themselves in court. Most of the inmates are drug addicts (about 40%), followers of the Falun Gong spiritual movement (28%) and prostitutes (about 10%).

I've heard about a guy called Liu Xiaobo, who's he?

Liu Xiaobo won the 2010 Nobel Peace prize. He is currently serving an 11 year jail sentence for "inciting subversion". That's the term the CCP uses if a person campaigns for political and human rights and/or an end to one-party rule.

In February 2010, a court in Chengdu handed out a five-year sentence to Tan Zuoren for "inciting subversion". His crime was to campaign on behalf of parents whose children had been killed when their shabbily built schools collapsed during an earthquake in 2008.

Some place! Why on earth was China given the 2008 Olympic Games?

You may well ask.

The International Olympic Committee expressed the hope that the Beijing Olympics would follow the example of the games in South Korea in 1988, where human rights and democracy improved through wider engagement with the world. The 1964 Tokyo Games were also a model, symbolising Japan's return to the world community, 19 years after its surrender in World War II.

Others believe this was, at best, naïve and at worst, cynical.

The Chinese economy, after all, has been hailed as the great economic miracle of our times. It is estimated that in the next three to four years, China will be richer than the entire 25 countries of the European Union put together. China makes 2/3 of the world's microwave ovens, 50% of our clothes, 50% of the world's cameras, 30% of our computers and 25% of our washing machines.

Even Scotland has pursued "enlightened self-interest". Scottish Ballet toured China in 2010. First Minister Alex Salmond visited China in 2009 to encourage Chinese students to study in our universities. He also promoted Scottish tourism (golf especially) and business links. The teaching of Mandarin is now established in many Scottish schools, as are "Confucius classrooms".

The CCP clearly feels the games were a great propaganda success, which they were. The stadia and the ceremonies were spectacular. 43 new world records and 132 new Olympic records were set. IOC President Jacques Rogge declared the event a "truly exceptional Games".

The human rights organisation, Amnesty International, claims that even in the immediate period running up to the Games, China broke its promises to uphold human rights. It claimed that China continued to persecute human rights activists, detain suspects without trial, censor the media and carry out the death penalty. It is noteworthy that China declined to bid for the 2018 or 2022 football World Cups. The football World Cup lasts four weeks, not two, and could present the kind of security challenges an authoritarian state such as China could not cope with.

How does China justify these human rights abuses?

The CCP has a different view of what constitutes "human rights" than the rest of the world! It believes that the "human rights of the many are more important than the human rights of a few". In other words, the millions taken out of poverty and the massive improvements in living standards for the vast majority of Chinese citizens are more important than free political activity. There is no doubt that the pace of change in China could not have taken place in a democratic society. China just does not do the kind of consultation, debate and scrutiny that is demanded in the UK.

Many Chinese themselves support this viewpoint. Of course, Communist and nationalist propaganda by a compliant media may well have played its part. On all the important issues, the Chinese media speaks with one voice – that of the Communist Party. But, protests do occur. In May 2010 a five day strike crippled car production at the Honda plant in Foshan, Guandong. This seriously worried the CCP, which ordered the media to limit coverage of it. The strikers won a 24% pay rise.

There was a 42% increase in labour disputes in Guangdong between 2008 and 2009. In Zehejiang province the increase was 160%. Workers have been winning the majority of these disputes, because the companies have been able to afford the pay rise, even the huge ones. So long as the economic miracle continues and living standards rise, protest against one party CCP rule will be limited.

Tell me a bit more about this "economic miracle"?

In 1979, Prime Minister Deng Xiaoping stated that "to get rich was glorious". Private enterprise and wealth were no longer incompatible with Chinese socialism. Deng's reforms have been continued by the current CCP leadership.

China's economy is aggressively capitalist. In the 1970s there was virtually no private sector to speak of in China. By 1998, 54% of China's economy was in private hands. In 2003, this figure was

71%. The number of state owned firms has fallen from 300,000 to 150,000 with millions of jobs lost in the process.

China has pursued inward investment from the major global brands, especially to its Special Enterprise Zones, where taxes and wages are low.

China has become the workshop of the world. The Chinese economy has experienced double digit growth for the past five years. Even the credit crunch has merely slowed down the pace of economic activity.

Unlike just about every other country in the world, China has not gone into recession. China has a population of 1,307,000,000 people. It has the largest workforce in the world. It is China alone, virtually, which has been responsible for any increases in living standards in Africa in the past ten years. China's demand for Africa's raw materials seems endless.

But, I thought there was a lot of poverty in China?

There is. Despite its claims to be a socialist society, China is one of the most unequal countries in the world.

The economic miracle has created many winners, but there are also many losers. According to an investigation published by the Chinese National Bureau of Statistics in June 2008, rich people, who make up 10% of China's population, control 45 per cent of the country's wealth. Poor people (those who earn less than $1 per day, 10% of the population), only control 1.4%. According to World Bank figures, there are 130 million poor people in China.

There is also the plight of migrant labourers, known as the "mingong". There are estimated to be between 150-200 million rural workers who have moved to China's cities in search of work and the number is set to grow. It is perhaps the biggest movement of people the world has ever seen. In some cities, migrants make up the majority of the population. The wages of migrant workers remain miserably low. Their average monthly salary is 780 yuan (£50).

Are there other social problems?

China's rapid industrialisation is causing environmental concerns. China's need to lift so many people out of poverty has been more important than long-term issues such as "sustainable development".

Waste pollution is the single most serious issue. As more people move into cities, the problem of household waste is becoming severe. Only 20% of China's 168m tonnes of solid waste per year is properly disposed of.

The air is not much better. According to the World Bank, China has 16 of the world's 20 most polluted cities. Estimates suggest that 300,000 people a year die prematurely from respiratory diseases.

The main reason is that around 70% of China's booming energy needs are supplied by coal-fired power stations, compared with 50% in America. Combined with the still widespread use of coal burners to heat homes, China has the world's highest emissions of sulphur dioxide and a quarter of the country endures acid rain.

The Three Gorges Dam on China's Yangtze River is the biggest hydroelectric dam ever built. The dam has destroyed forest and aquatic habitat, submerged archaeological sites and displaced millions of people from their homes. Thirteen new towns have been built to house the evicted families and industries. Critics claim these effects were brushed off while the project was being planned.

China says it needs alternative energy sources to combat widespread power shortages and keep its booming economy powering along. The CCP also says the dam was necessary to prevent further flooding in the Yangtze, which has claimed thousands of lives.

Study Theme 3C
The United States of America

Need to know

➤ How the US political system works
➤ Trends in participation and representation in political life
➤ Differences and similarities between different political parties
➤ The immigration debate
➤ Social and economic inequalities among and within the USA's racial groups
➤ Government social/economic strategies

Background

The USA is a nation of immigrants. Only American Indians, or "native Americans" as they are now known, can trace their ancestry to this land. They now make up around only 1% of the population.

Europeans were attracted to the USA for greater economic opportunities or to escape famine or war. The USA expanded southward, taking land from neighbouring Mexico, which explains the country's large Latino population. Mexico and its neighbouring central American countries are poor. The immigration debate is a controversial one within the USA.

The slave trade brought Africans to America. An estimated 15 million Africans were transported to the Americas between 1540 and 1850. Even with a death rate of 50%, merchants could still expect to make a profit from the trade.

The notion of the American Dream is very important to the nation's psyche. Americans, in general, like to believe that hard work and enterprise will have its reward.

Because the nation has many freedoms and opportunities, there is not the same welfare support available for those who are not financially independent.

While the two main political parties, Democrats and Republicans are very different, both share the ideology of the American Dream; individual responsibility, civic duty and patriotism. Americans are very proud of the country's tradition of free speech. American radio, especially, and now the internet, are the arenas for the "culture war" between conservatives, e.g. Rush Limbaugh and liberals e.g. Michael Moore.

Liberals tend to be "pro-choice" on abortion issues, in favour of gun control, gay marriage, state or "social" health care, and are more pragmatic in their religious views. Conservatives, the opposite on them all! The American people have the choice!

Does the USA have a written Constitution?

The Constitution is the supreme law of the United States. It has seven articles covering how the country should be governed and the rights of its citizens. There have been seventeen amendments, the most famous, perhaps, being the 1st, which guarantees freedom of religion and free speech and the 2nd, which gives citizens the right to possess firearms. Most Americans take these seven articles very seriously and many can recite them off by heart!

What are checks and balances?

The framers of the Constitution were very careful that no one person or no one part of Government should be all-powerful.

As such, in the USA there are a whole set of elaborate checks and balances to make sure that neither the executive (President), the legislature (Congress) or the judiciary (Supreme Court) can become over powerful. For example, the President cannot declare war without Congressional approval. In the UK the Prime Minister can declare war and need not have a vote in the House of Commons.

Congress can reject a Presidential bill. The President can veto Congressional legislation, but a 2/3 majority in both Houses can over-turn the President's veto.

The President can nominate Supreme Court judges, but only when there is a vacancy. The Senate has to approve Presidential nominations.

Is the President all-powerful?

Certainly not. The classic definition of Presidential power in the United States is that of political scientist Richard Neustadt.

Writing in the 1970s, he described presidential power in the United States as *"not the power to command, but the power to persuade."*

In truth, the President has more than a few constitutional and extra constitutional cards to play. It is perhaps in foreign policy that the President's powers are strongest. The moment he is sworn into office, the President becomes the Commander in Chief of the US military, the most powerful force in the world.

Only Congress can declare war. But, the "Commander in Chief" can initiate military action abroad without a formal declaration of war.

The President can also make treaties with other countries (subject to 2/3 of the Senate agreeing). Current military campaigns are, of course, Operation Iraqi Freedom and Operation Enduring Freedom: Afghanistan.

The President can nominate members of the Supreme Court, positions the incumbents occupy for life. However, the Senate must approve these nominations, and in the past this has been a stumbling block. However, Barack Obama has been able to successfully nominate two Supreme Court judges in his two years in power: Sonia Sotomayor and Elena Kagan.

Are there any examples of the President not getting everything his own way?Lots. President George W Bush was forced to use the Presidential veto after Congress rejected his Iraq War Funds Bill. A President can only serve two terms in office. Once the President enters his last years as President he often loses his authority and becomes a "lame duck" president. Congress, depending on its political make up, can become more assertive over the President. President Bush had to resort to his veto on other issues such as torture of terrorist suspects and stem cell research.

Because of the Republican wins in the 2010 mid-term elections, President Obama may find it difficult to secure funds from Congress for his health care reforms. In December 2010, the Senate blocked President Obama's DREAM Act, a proposal which would have given children brought to the U.S. illegally a chance of residency if they attended college or served in the military.

What about the Supreme Court?

It is the Supreme Court, rather than the President or the Congress, which has been responsible for some of the most significant reforms to life in the USA. Brown v the Board of Education in 1954 ended racially segregated schooling. Roe v Wade in 1973 legalised abortion. The Supreme Court ruled that the imprisonment of terrorist suspects at Guantanamo Bay was illegal, much to President Bush's dismay. The Supreme Court remains the focus of many pressure groups on issues such as affirmative action or same sex marriages.

What is meant by federalism?

The USA is a federation of 50 states who have agreed to join together as one country. The Federal Government in Washington DC runs the country but many laws are de-centralised to the 50 states.

Each of the states takes its identity very seriously. The Civil War of 1861-1865 involved the breakaway states of the South who believed slavery was an issue for states to decide, not the federal government. Laws differ between the states on, for example, capital punishment, marriage, the legal age to drink alcohol and many more issues. Each state has its own state congress and "President", who is known as the state Governor.

Who are the Republicans?

Former President George W Bush was a Republican. The best known Republican at the moment is probably Sarah Palin. Traditionally the Republican Party is supported by big business.

The Republicans are opposed to "big Government" and support issues such as low taxes and free trade. The problem is taxes have been cut, worker protections have been reduced, and the free market has been given a freer hand.

After the banking crisis and the credit crunch, many ordinary Americans are sceptical about big business running America. But, they are also distrustful of the Government!

This explains the backlash against President Obama in the 2010 mid-term elections and the rise of the Republican pressure group, the Tea Party. The Tea Party is diverse in nature but rallies around tax cuts, less government and, especially, opposition to "socialised medical care".

While the Tea Party claims to be a "grass roots" movement, of normal citizens, there is evidence that it is financially supported by traditional big money. In this respect it is an "astroturf movement" as well as a grassroots one. The Tea Party came from nowhere to become a very powerful voice force in the Republican Party.

Who are the Democrats?

President Barack Obama is a Democrat. Democrats, in general, tend to be more liberal on social issues and believe in a bigger role for government in the economy, for example, in providing health insurance.

The trade unions in America are a strong base of support for the Democrats. The Democrats are much more likely to support workers rights and issues such as the national minimum wage. Racial minorities, especially African Americans are strong supporters of the Democrats.

Who votes for who?

The much discussed group of voters known as "middle America" are the group who will switch between Democrat and Republican, depending, usually on the state of the economy or a general "feel-good" factor behind a candidate. Especially in Presidential elections, but in other elections too, Americans take the personal qualities of a politician perhaps a bit more seriously than we do.

The most recent set of elections in the USA, the 2010-mid term elections, saw the Republicans bounce back into Government. But, the results confirmed certain long-term trends too.

Overall, across the USA, the richer and better educated are more likely to vote Republican. Of those who earn more than $100,000 per year, 58% voted Republican. 40% voted Democrat.

Men are much more likely to vote Republican than women. Able bodied white men are the only group in the USA who do not benefit from affirmative action programmes, which Republicans tend to oppose. Republicans, in general, are opposed to "political correctness", for example minority rights, something white males are more likely to oppose too.

Young voters are much more likely to vote Democrat. 56% of 18-29 year olds voted Democrat. Unfortunately for the Democrats, young voters make up just 11% of the electorate.

African Americans are the Democrats most faithful supporters. 90% of African Americans vote democrat. Hispanics are, in general, Democrat supporters too, but not to the same degree. 65% of Hispanics voted Democrat in 2010. The civil rights struggles of the 1950s and 1960s cemented the relationship between Democrats and African Americans. Hispanics, more ethnically, financially and geographically diverse, have a less loyal relationship to the Democrats. Republican opposition to immigration has influenced many Hispanics to vote Democrat.

What are the issues over immigration?

The 1990 Immigration Act (IMMACT) limits the annual number of immigrants to 700,000. Controversy has arisen over existing immigration law and immigration outside the law, especially over the 7.5 million illegal alien workers with more than 12 million household members already inside the U.S. Another 700,000 to 850,000 are predicted to enter each coming year.

Mexico is a pressing issue. Roughly half of Mexico's population lives on less than $5 a day. The federal US minimum wage is $7.25 *an hour*. It's not hard to see the attraction of "El Norte".

President George W Bush attempted to neutralise the immigration issue with his Immigration Bill of 2006-07. "Operation Jumpstart" was his plan to solve the immigration problem. Like much else of Bush's domestic agenda, the President ran into Congressional opposition and the bill ultimately failed in June 2007. He did though succeed in using the National Guard to patrol the US/Mexico border.

Strength of feeling on the issue was illustrated in March 2006 when hundreds of thousands of activists marched in California to protest against plans to criminalise undocumented workers.

The Day Without Immigrants protest was a day when legal and some illegal immigrants stopped work to show the contribution immigrants make to America.

Are immigrants a drain on resources?

Some people argue this, particularly those who live in border states. According to the Federation for American Immigration Reform, California's education system spends $7.7 billion each year caring for the children of illegal immigrants.

On the other hand, it is highly unlikely that many businesses in Southern California, especially, could cope without immigrants.

That was the essential message of the Day Without Immigrants protest. Vineyards, restaurants, housemaids, cleaners, and other low paid insecure jobs are carried out by illegal immigrants, often paid less than minimum wage, with no holiday or sick pay.

What's the latest situation?

Immigration occasionally flares up as a political issue. This is one of these moments. Arizona's state law on immigration, SB1070, signed on April 23 2010, makes illegal immigration a state misdemeanour (in addition to being a federal civil violation).

It empowers local police to make "lawful contact" in order to check the immigration status of people who cause "reasonable suspicion" and to arrest them if they lack documents. To the Hispanic community, this, in effect, means that Hispanic looking drivers will be pulled over by the police on potentially any pretext.

There is the possibility that other states, notably New Mexico and Texas, could follow Arizona's lead. On the other hand, pro-immigration groups have been mobilised. There have been boycotts of the state and private companies have cancelled conferences. "Your Vote is Your Voice", is the slogan of the Southwest Voter Registration Education Project (SVREEP). Antonio Gonzalez of SVREEP says that SB1070 has made the Hispanic lobby "100 times larger than the Tea Party".

President Obama has promised "comprehensive reform" of immigration and while criticising Arizona, acknowledges the lack of federal action on immigration has encouraged actions such as SB1070. He has stated that illegal immigrants need a "pathway to legal status".

Competition for jobs is rising with unemployment. If President Obama doesn't move fast in 2010, reform could become an election issue in 2012. If the US economy is still in recession, immigration could be a vote winner for Republicans tapping into xenophobic feeling. Failure to act could lose him the support of the millions of Hispanics who voted for him and the Democrats in 2008.

What about race? Is the American dream open to everyone, regardless of race?

The USA is probably more meritocratic now than it ever was. The election of Barack Obama as President was symbolic more than anything else. But symbols are important. Few African Americans who were hosed off the streets in Alabama or set upon by dogs in Mississippi could have thought they'd live to see the day when a black man was President.

Four decades ago, there were only 300 black elected officials nationwide and three African-American members of Congress. Today there are around 9,000 black elected officials (BEOs). These include Supreme Court judges, Congressmen, Governors and cabinet members.

Economically, blacks have benefited from the advances made during the Civil Rights era. The racial disparity in poverty rates has narrowed. The black middle class has grown substantially. In 2000, 47% of African Americans owned their homes.

In 2004, African American workers had the second-highest median earnings of American minority groups after Asian Americans. In 2001, over half of African American households of married couples earned $50,000 or more.

A black middle class, helped in part by Affirmative Action, has emerged. About 1.1m blacks earn over $100,000 a year. But, there are still great inequalities. A 2009 survey by researchers at Brandeis University, Mass, found that a typical white family is five times richer than its African-American counterpart. Only 1 in 10 African-Americans owns any shares. A third do not have a pension plan and among those who do, the value is, on average, a fifth of that of whites.

Segregation no longer has the force of law, but it is still a fact of life in most cities. Many school districts are actually going backwards in terms of their social and racial mix. High-income and middle-class white parents are using the housing market to buy a better education for their children. They have moved in droves to suburban school districts that are outside the city. Other affluent families have quit the public system entirely, and use private schools instead.

In many American cities, especially in the north-east and Midwest, middle-class parents can choose from a variety of separate districts in nearby suburbs, leaving struggling cities behind. Detroit, for example, has been left with one of America's starkest racial divides between city and suburbs, and the quality of the city's public schools has collapsed.

What about poverty?

Poverty rates for blacks and Hispanics greatly exceed the national average. In 2009, 25.8% of blacks and 25.3 % of Hispanics were poor, compared to 9.4 % of non-Hispanic whites and 12.5% of Asians. The poverty threshold in the USA is an annual income of $21,756 for two adults and two children.

Curiously, despite the numbers of Hispanics living in poverty, a Hispanic person born in 2006 can expect to live to the ripe old age of about 80 years, more than 2 years longer than non-Hispanic whites. Average black life expectancy is 73 years. One reason put forward for this is that moving from one country to another takes some effort and fitness. So the United States may be attracting relatively healthier people from Mexico, the largest source of Hispanic immigrants.

What about crime? Is it true that a young black male is more likely to go to jail than university?

More or less. While only 13% of the US population is African American, African Americans make up 50% of the prison population.

There are several reasons for this. Crack cocaine, which is more likely to be used by African-Americans, will trigger felony charges for amounts 100 times less than powdered cocaine, which is more likely to be used by whites.

Racial profiling has been shown to target African-Americans for police stops and searches. And drug dealing is more likely to be out in the open in poor communities, but behind closed doors in suburbs. Poverty and dysfunctional family life are other contributory factors. Does the glamourisation of crime by rappers play its part too?

Will there be an Obama effect in the years to come? Can the message of "Yes We Can" cross over to wider social and economic African American life?

Does the US Government try to help those who don't have the American Dream?

In the immediate aftermath of the credit crunch, President Barack Obama sought to save the American economy. In February 2009, the US Senate approved President Obama's fiscal stimulus package of $787 billion in tax cuts and cuts in public spending. Yet, the recovery remains fragile. Unemployment remains high at around 10%. Business confidence is low, and house prices have yet to recover.

While US Governments, in general, believe it is up to individuals and families to provide for themselves, there is state support for those less well off.

The 'Welfare to Work' (Personal Responsibility and Work Opportunity Reconciliation Act – PRWORA) is the main government strategy to reduce poverty in USA. The poor are expected to 'work their way out of poverty', and federal and state governments have a variety of benefits such as Medicaid health insurance, child care, food stamps, and Earned Income Tax Credit which is dependent upon the individual actively seeking work.

The state-run (but federal financed) Temporary Assistance to Needy Families (TANF) is the main program to reduce child poverty. Welfare benefits are linked to finding work or training for work. The US grants individuals a maximum of five years welfare payments in a lifetime.

A variety of housing subsidy programmes are available to lower income households.

President Obama has, of course, recently passed his health care reforms which will grant all American citizens health care insurance. Tea Party Republicans have vowed not to grant him the funds to implement the policy.

Study Theme 3E The Politics of Development

Need to know

➤ The economic, political and social factors which affect development

➤ The links between health, education, food and development

➤ Roles of governments: Africa, African Union (AU), European Union (EU), United Nations (UN), the UK and Non-Governmental Organisations (NGOs) in promoting development

➤ For this Study Theme, reference must be made to a specific African country (but not South Africa). Specific, real, up to date examples of an African nation you know well are far preferable to a tokenistic mention of some random country you know little about.

Background: the UN Millennium Goals

• Poverty & Hunger
• Child Mortality
• Gender
• HIV, AIDS, Malaria and other diseases
• Aid, Trade, Growth & Global Partnership
• Maternal health
• Education
• Environment

In 2010, the UN reported on progress made towards the goals as part of its five year audit. The overall conclusions were that five years away from the 2015 deadline to achieve the Millennium Development Goals (MDGs), despite many successes, overall progress has been too slow for most of the targets to be met by 2015. Here are some extracts from the report on progress with some of the goals:

Target 1: Halve the proportion of people living on less than $1 a day.

All developing regions *except sub-Saharan Africa*, western Asia and parts of Eastern Europe, are expected to achieve the MDG target.

Because of the international recession, in sub-Saharan Africa both the number of poor and the poverty rate are expected to increase in some of the more vulnerable and low-growth economies.

TARGET 2: Ensure that, by 2015, children everywhere, boys and girls alike, will be able to complete a full course of primary schooling.

The abolition of primary fees in Burundi has enabled enrolment to reach 99%. Similarly Tanzania and Zambia have broken through the 90% threshold. *But the pace of progress is insufficient.*

TARGET 3: Eliminate gender disparity in primary and secondary education, preferably by 2005, and in all levels of education no later than 2015.

Gender parity in primary and secondary schools *in sub-Saharan Africa is unlikely to be achieved*.

TARGET 4: Reduce by two thirds, between 1990 and 2015, the under-five mortality rate.

Child mortality rates are falling. *But not quickly enough to meet the target.* 1 in 7 children in sub-Saharan Africa die before their 5th birthday.

TARGET 5: Reduce by three quarters, between 1990 and 2015, the maternal mortality ratio.

Progress was made in all regions, but was especially dramatic in Northern Africa and South-Eastern Asia, with increases of 74%

and 63% respectively. Southern Asia also progressed, although coverage there, as well as in *sub-Saharan Africa, remains inadequate*. Less than half the women giving birth in these regions are attended by skilled health personnel.

TARGET 6: Have halted by 2015 and begun to reverse the spread of HIV/AIDS, malaria and other diseases.

AIDS-related mortality peaked in 2004, with 2.2 million deaths. *Sub-Saharan Africa remains the most heavily affected region*, accounting for 72% of all new infections in 2008. The growing availability of drugs to control HIV, treat malaria and measles brings hope that this target can be reached. Tuberculosis remains the second biggest killer after HIV.

Target 7: Halve, by 2015, the proportion of the population without sustainable access to safe drinking water and basic sanitation.

While the world as a whole is on target to meet the MDG target, *only 60% of Sub-Saharan Africa has access to clean drinking water*. 64% lack access to basic sanitation and this target is likely to be missed.

TARGET 8: Deal comprehensively with developing countries' debt.

The debt burden has eased for developing nations and remains well below historic levels.

But aid remains well below the UN target of 0.7% of gross national income. In 2009, the only countries to reach or exceed the target were Denmark, Luxembourg, the Netherlands, Norway and Sweden.

Are African nations not to blame for the state they are in?

Poor governance by African nations is certainly an issue. But other factors have played their part too. Not all African nations are the same. You wouldn't generalise about European countries' political systems. African nations all have their own histories, political cultures and specific social/economic issues.

Take colonialism, for example. The UK, France, Belgium, Holland and other European countries plundered Africa's natural resources for centuries and stunted their development. Many African countries did not gain their independence until after World War 2.

Zimbabwe used to be known as Rhodesia, after the (in) famous, depending on your point of view, "explorer" Cecil Rhodes. Colonialism left behind a land tenure structure which left most of the best land in the hands of large, commercial farms. Poor, black families were concentrated in the least fertile land, mostly on tiny land holdings. Black Zimbabweans worked on the land, but had no property rights and, crucially, few skills in managing the complex business of agriculture. Colonialism also left behind an economy which was dependent on cash crops. In Zimbabwe's case, maize and tobacco. If anything happens to these two crops, the Zimbabwean economy will always be in real trouble. It has and it is.

White-only rule in Zimbabwe ended as recently as 1980 when Robert Mugabe of the Zimbabwe African National Union (ZANU-PF) became the country's leader. Mr Mugabe and his party have ruled Zimbabwe ever since.

Mugabe has promised to rule until he is 100. In February 2009, Opposition leader Morgan Tsvangirai joined the new Inclusive Government of Zimbabwe. The coalition has been a fragile one, with Mugabe keen to retain his supporters in important positions.

Zimbabwe is a fascinating, and disturbing, example of development. Zimbabwe, used to be known as the "bread basket of Africa". It was, and should be, a thriving, prosperous nation. But Zimbabwe has one of the lowest life expectancies in the world. The average Zimbabwean can only expect to live to 43 years of age.

Why?
Bad governance is the main reason. Between 2005 and 2008, Zimbabwe suffered economic meltdown, characterised by shortages of foreign currency, electricity, fuel, food, medicine and basic commodities.

In August 2006, Zimbabwe scrapped the old currency and brought in a new one. Most people stashed bags of money at home as the prices of goods and services climbed almost every few days. Others, people who live around shopping centres went on shopping sprees, with some spending as much as $300 million on an assortment of goods. In February 2009, inflation in Zimbabwe was estimated at 10 sextillion% (10 to the power of 21), the highest in the world.

Even Zimbabwe's ruling elite struggled. It is reported that when playing golf, they had to buy their drinks before they teed off. The drink prices would have doubled by the time they finished their round!

In 2009, the Inclusive Government introduced the US dollar as the nation's currency. Mugabe rules Zimbabwe through terror. He was re-elected President in 2008, in a controversial one-man race.

Morgan Tsvangirai, leader of the opposition party, the Movement for Democratic Change (MDC), pulled out of the run-off election, saying its supporters were being attacked and killed. Tsvangira had been beaten up by Mugabe's supporters in a previous Presidential election.

What bad policies has Mugabe's government pursued?

Land reform for one. In November 2001 Mugabe's Government embarked on a "fast track" policy of land redistribution. In effect, this meant the farms of white farmers were violently taken by friends and supporters of Mugabe's ruling political party. The country was thrown into complete chaos.

These farms which used to be the country's main foreign exchange earner now lie empty or are used as second homes by Mugabe's political supporters. Mugabe and his wife, Grace, have occupied 12 of the most productive farms. This is known as "kleptocracy", when Government Ministers steal the nation's resources for personal gain.

Any other examples of kleptocracy?

Mugabe remains determined to loot Zimbabwe for his supporters.

In 2010, without consulting his MDC coalition partners, Mugabe passed a new law which forces private companies to give black Zimbabweans a 51% stake in their companies. This has been a disaster for inward investment.

Mugabe is also desperate to profit from the country's Marange diamond field, reputed to be the biggest diamond find in the history of mankind. Potential revenue is estimated at $1 billion-$1.7 billion a year; about half of Zimbabwe's total forecast GDP this year and enough to end its economic woes almost at a stroke.

The Kimberley Process Certification Scheme, which regulates international diamond trade, currently bans Zimbabwe from trading due to Zanu-PF human rights abuses and corruption. Mugabe is working hard to have the ban overturned.

How bad are things in Zimbabwe?

The unemployment rate in Zimbabwe is 94%. In the UK it's 7%. Gross Domestic product per head in Zimbabwe (what we earn in a year) is £132. In the UK it's £20,048. 85 infants per 1,000 die in Zimbabwe. Just 6 children in the UK per 1,000 die as infants. The adult HIV/AIDS rate in Zimbabwe is 20.1%. In the UK it is 0.2%.

Mr Mugabe, himself, at the remarkable age of 86, is in rude health.

What is the world doing about this?

The UK's aid agency, the Department for International Development (DFID), tries to help Zimbabwe's people, not the Zimbabwean government. It will work with UN agencies such as the Food and Agricultural organisation (FAO), World Health Organisation (WHO) or recognised NGOs, such as Oxfam, to assist the most needy. In 2009, total UK aid to Zimbabwe amounted to £90m, the largest sum ever. No funds went to or through the Government of Zimbabwe.

Mugabe's Zimbabwe was the first elected government to be excluded from the Commonwealth for contravening the democratic principles agreed at the 1991 Harare conference. In 2004, Zimbabwe formally resigned from the Commonwealth. The International Monetary Fund (IMF) will not provide Zimbabwe with financial aid until the Government pays its $1.3 billion arrears to the World Bank.

Ok, bad governance is certainly a factor. Are there any other reasons for African nations being poor?

Bad governance often forces the most talented people to leave

114

African countries, making the problems even worse. This is known as the brain drain.

Many of Africa's top professionals leave their countries to come and work in developed nations. Health workers especially, are in great need in African nations, but these workers can earn much higher salaries in the UK or the USA.

According to a report by the Pollution Research Group at Natal University in South Africa, Africa lost an estimated 60,000 middle- and high-level managers between 1985 and 1990, and about 23,000 qualified academic professionals emigrate each year in search of better working conditions.

While sub-Saharan Africa it has 11% of the world's population and 24 % of the global burden of disease, it has only 3% of the world's health workers. Ethiopia has a population of more than 73 million. In April 2007, there were only 108 surgeons in the country and 15 anaesthesiologists. There are more Ethiopian doctors in Chicago than there are in Ethiopia.

What about third world debt?

Debt is an important factor too.

According to the NGO, Jubilee 2000, Kenya, with an average life expectancy of 48 years and an average income per head of $481, gives $364 million each year to the rich world in debt payments. Its annual spending on health care is $430 million a year.

There are many reasons for the debt crisis, both political and economic. Development campaigners have argued that the rules on debt, aid and trade need reforming to help lift more African nations out of poverty.

During the Cold War, corrupt African leaders were often able to gain financing from major powers anxious to retain their loyalty. The creditors received what they paid for -- support in the Cold War. Yet the debt burden remained for future generations to pay.

In the 1960s and 1970s, international lenders readily pushed a high volume of loans on many African states. Neither the lenders nor the borrowers anticipated how high the cost of repayment would rise. For African countries with agricultural exports, both unpredictable prices and natural disasters increased vulnerability to debt, just as for farmers anywhere in the world. World oil price hikes in 1972 and 1979 dramatically raised the cost of imports. Even countries that exported oil and other minerals faced boom and bust cycles that raised the odds of incurring unsustainable debt. When interest rates skyrocketed in the 1980s, interest payments jumped. Trying to pay off more debt with less income allowed unpaid debt to mushroom. With all these factors at work, the impact of every additional mistake in economic policy was multiplied.

What about terms of trade?

The unfair terms of trade is another important factor.

The European Union's Common Agricultural Policy puts high tariffs on many imports from poor countries. At the same time, it subsidises exports of surplus produce from Europe, undermining the livelihoods of many African farmers.

Anti poverty campaigners stress that, while debt relief is important, as are other forms of aid, having fairer trade with African nations is perhaps the best way to help end poverty.

This has sparked the growth of the Fair Trade Movement by NGOs. In 1994 there were just three fair trade products on the market in the UK. Now there are more than 2,000 – including coffee and chocolate – on sale in Scottish shops and supermarkets. Former First Minister Jack McConnell committed Scotland to becoming a Fair Trade nation.

Armed conflicts can't help either?

No. Africa consistently remains among the top places for ongoing conflicts, consisting of both long standing civil wars and conflicts between countries. Financing war often comes before economic development.

During the period 1956 to 2001, Africa experienced 156 coups d'etats (overthrow of the government by the military). Since 1956, over seven million Africans have been directly killed in war. The war in Chad lasted for forty years.

The civil war in Darfur, in the west of Sudan, has claimed some 400,000 lives. The President of the country, Omar al-Bashir, has backed an Arab militia, the Janjaweed, to flush out, by violent means, the rebels who operate from the midst of southern farmers.

There have been gruesome reports of torture, rapes and murders. Women and children appear to be targeted by the Janjaweed for brutal attacks.

Can international bodies not help?

Increasingly UN agencies work together with national aid agencies (the UK's aid agency is DFID) and recognised NGOs. DFID will partly fund UN agencies such as UNICEF and FAO, and the work of the UN World Food Programme. DFID also gives money to organisations such as the IMF or the World Bank for their development programmes.

A good example is the UK's work with Malawi. DFID has worked closely with the government of Malawi. Malawi now has a more democratic government and DFID will work alongside it to promote development. Scotland also has many development projects in Malawi. (Scots were among the first "explorers" in the country). Working with the Scotland/ Malawi Partnership, pupils from Glasgow's Holyrood Secondary School raised a staggering £70,000 to fund a visit to Malawi to re-furbish two schools in Blantyre, Malawi. Sir Tom Hunter has set up a foundation to fund development in Malawi.

DFID's 14 priority countries are Democratic Republic of Congo, Ethiopia, Ghana, Kenya, Malawi, Mozambique, Sierra Leone, Nigeria, Rwanda, Sudan, Tanzania, Uganda, Zambia and Zimbabwe.

The vast bulk of DFID's money goes on reducing poverty in Africa. In 2007/08, DFID spent approximately £1.17 billion on bilateral and regional programmes to reduce poverty in Africa. Before it left office in 2010, the UK Labour Government enshrined in law a commitment to raise UK aid spending to 0.7% of GDP by 2013, a pledge that will involve the budget of DFID increasing by more than 10% a year.

The African Union (AU) has been modelled on the same lines as the European Union (EU). The AU seeks to resolve Africa's many wars, assist the flow of trade across its borders, and allow Africa to speak with one voice in world affairs.

But, the AU has yet to make a decisive contribution. In June 2008, the AU refused to condemn Robert Mugabe's conduct during the Zimbabwean Presidential election and endorsed his Presidency.

In 2009, the AU refused to co-operate with the UN International Criminal Court when it charged Sudan President Omar al-Bashir with crimes against humanity.

What about the G8 and G20 countries? Did they not promise to cut debt and increase aid?

The 2005 Gleneagles G8 summit was unique in that it required G8 leaders to sign up to a series of specific measures. The G8 promised to increase overall aid spending by $50 billion by 2010. It promised to make Aids treatment free, provide universal access to free primary education and health care.

But keeping the commitments – and the funding needed for them – has been harder than making them. All G8 countries have suffered from the credit crunch and recession. The UK has been one of the better nations at cutting debt and increasing aid. The Organisation for Economic Co-operation and Development (OECD) reported that less than half the money promised to Africa at the 2005 Gleneagles G8 summit has been provided. At the 2010 G20 conference in Toronto, Prime Minister David Cameron criticised his fellow world leaders for not keeping their promises to Africa.

What about NGOs?

The term "non-government organization" was first used at the founding of the UN in 1948. It implies that there is a distance between NGOs and government. The reality is that NGOs have a great deal of contact with governments.

In the first place, it is NGOs on the ground which often see to the delivery of food, planned by national and international government. There is a *partnership* at work.

NGOs are often funded by governments. Around one quarter of Oxfam's funds come from the UK and EU governments. Without the funding by Governments, many NGOs could not exist. This is a relationship which suits governments. A government may respect an NGO and realise that it can manage and deliver an aid project more efficiently than government. NGOs can be cheaper and more efficient than bilateral, government to government aid.

NGOs have achieved many great things. At their best, NGOs bring foreign expertise to impoverished areas and teach locals sustainable agricultural methods.

They employ local people and have precise goals which are monitored and are achievable. Oxfam is a highly regarded NGO. As is the Scottish based Football4life. They are both campaigners and aid providers, delivering both short and long term changes.

Do NGOs not have their disadvantages too?

Not all NGOs are the same. Just like government organisations, some non-government organisations are better than others.

It is alleged that some do not adhere to the Red Cross Code that they "respect culture and custom", instead lobbying for western values, for example feminism, in societies which may have a male dominated culture.

NGOs are unelected. They are, despite their best intentions, unaccountable to anyone for their actions. If official British government funds have gone to the wrong people, the Government will be held to account and the Minister responsible put on the spot. But NGOs are private organizations, responsible only to themselves.

NGOs may also inadvertently prolong wars or complicate wars. They may feed warring armies, complicating the foreign policy of the British government. Bigger NGOs, especially, can bring Western salaries, personnel and purchasing power into a poor country, which can have an adverse effect on local markets, causing inflation and resentment.

Study Theme 3F Global Security

What is the UN's main role?

The UN's main job in terms of global security is to keep the peace and resolve conflict as soon as possible. But the main UN organ responsible for this, the Security Council, is often ineffective due to internal squabbling, long-running debates about its membership and doubts over its very legitimacy

When the UN does act, it often fails to provide its peacekeepers with the means to accomplish their missions. Genocide has occurred in Rwanda, the Balkans and Sudan. The UN stood by as thousands of innocent civilians were slaughtered.

The Sudanese Government, responsible for the murder of its black citizens, retains a seat on the United Nations Human Rights Commission.

In 2002, the oil-for-food scandal involved the son of former UN leader Kofi Annan in a £10 billion swindle. In 2003, the UN was powerless to prevent the US and its allies from invading Iraq. The

UN International Atomic Energy Authority has somehow managed to miss Iran acquiring the capacity to develop nuclear weaponry.

More recently, the UN, perhaps unfairly, has been criticised for not being able to stop the terror and bloodshed in the Democratic Republic of Congo (DRC).

The organisation has enjoyed more success in its other, wider, roles, The UN's charter commits the organisation to safeguard human rights, to provide a mechanism for international law, to promote social and economic progress, and improve living standards and fight diseases. Countless lives have been saved through the work of agencies such as the WHO and the FAO or through improved education via UNESCO.

But these issues are outwith our Study Theme. We are concerned with the UN and its effectiveness in maintaining peace and security.

What are the main institutions of the UN?

First of all, there is the UN General Assembly. This is its main forum for debate. All member countries are represented. All countries have one vote and a 2/3 majority is required for resolution to succeed. The General Assembly appoints the UN Secretary General, currently Ban Ki-Moon.

Ban Ki-moon is up for re-election in 2011. He is likely to be re-elected for another 5 years term, largely because the US likes a low-key UN Secretary General.

But, while some accept that his style of leadership is different from western expectations, there has been criticism that Ban Ki-moon is simply not up to the task of reforming the UN and tackling the many problems the world faces. In particular, The 2009 Copenhagen Climate Change talks, in which he placed a great deal of his credibility, were a failure. He has been termed "the UN's invisible leader".

Secondly, there is the UN Security Council. Its primary responsibility is to maintain peace. It can be convened at any time if a member state feels there is an international crisis. Decisions are mandatory on all UN member states. The Security Council has 15 members with 1 vote each; five permanent members – UK, USA, France, Russian Federation, China and other ten elected by the Assembly for a two year term. Permanent members have the power of veto.

Decision making requires nine yes votes; including all permanent members. The Security Council can enforce decisions through sanctions and authorise military action as a last resort.

Thirdly, there is the International Court of Justice. In March 2010 Radovan Karadic eventually appeared before the international court. Karadzic is charged with genocide, complicity in genocide, extermination, murder, wilful killing, persecutions, deportation and inhumane acts against Muslims, Croats and other non-Serb civilians. His trial continues.

What are the UN's big successes?

It is much easier to point to failures of the UN than to look at its successes. The UN's greatest achievements are to be found in economic and social development, via FAO and WHO or through refugee work done by UNHCR or UNICEF.

There have been a total of 64 UN peacekeeping missions since 1948. Currently there are 15 active missions. The mission in the Democratic Republic of Congo is just one example. While, as always, the "blue helmets" are hampered by a lack of resources, there is no doubt that without the UN troops the carnage and suffering would be off the scale.

This leads us to the question, what would happen in the world if the UN was not there? There would be no neutral body to broker peace agreements. One country could dominate the world. While there have been many armed conflicts around the world, there has been no repeat of the two world wars which occurred immediately prior to the UN being set up. Surely the UN can take some credit for the fact that nuclear weaponry has not been used since Nagasaki in 1945?

Any failureThe failures are much easier to identify.

Rwanda 1994. In 1994 Rwanda's president, Juvenal Habyarimana, was assassinated, and an existing civil war between the two main ethnic groups, the Hutu and the Tutsi, turned into a campaign of genocide.

Around 800,000 people, mainly Tutsis, were murdered in 100 days. Western powers could have used force to end the killing. Romeo Dallaire, the UN's chief soldier in Rwanda, said it would have taken only 5,000 troops.

Srebrenica 1995. The 1992-1995 war in Bosnia claimed around 230,000 lives and created more than 2 million refugees.

In 1995, the UN "safe haven" of Srebrenica was being guarded by 200 Dutch UN peacekeepers. The Muslims gathered inside were afraid of massacre by the Serb army. They were right to be concerned. Around 7,000 people were murdered by the Serbs.

UN peacekeepers, the so-called "blue helmets" stood by, the Dutch having indicated that it was not worth risking their troops to defend the Muslims. Then UN Secretary-General, Kofi Annan, described the massacre at Srebrenica as *"scenes from hell, written on the darkest pages of human history"*. The conflict only ended when NATO used air strikes, without Security Council backing, to bring the war to an end.

Iraq 2003. The UN's authority was badly undermined by President Bush's decision to invade Iraq in 2003. Bush hoped for a new UN resolution to invade, after weapons inspectors could not find weapons of mass destruction (WMD). But, he could not achieve one.

The US justified its actions under international law by referring to Article 51 of the UN Constitution which allows a state to use force in "self defence", if it believes it is about to come under attack. In plain language, this allows a country to "retaliate first". President Bush and Prime Minister Tony Blair claimed that Iraq was planning an attack on the US and the UK. The UN was powerless to prevent the war.

The war in Iraq succeeded in overthrowing, and executing, former President Saddam Hussein. But no weapons of mass destruction were ever found. It is estimated that anything between 100,000 – 600,000 Iraqi civilians have been killed as a result of the war. Over 4,000 US troops have been killed. And they are not home yet.

Iraq now has its own democratically elected Government. But, is the US, and the UK for that matter, still seen as the great enemy by Muslims in the middle east?

Sudan 2003 – present. There has been a civil war in Darfur since 2003. The Janjaweed militia, allegedly supported by the Sudanese government, have been attacking the non-Arab population, intent on ethnic cleansing. More than two million people have been displaced from their homes since 2004 and are living in makeshift shelters in temporary camps. Women and young girls who leave the camps to collect fire wood are often vulnerable to attack from the Janjaweed.

China, a veto-wielding member of the Security Council with strong economic interests in Sudan, has backed its ally and made the UN mandate weaker than it could have been. The International Criminal Court has charged Sudan President Omar al-Bashir) with crimes against humanity. He has simply refused to turn up.

What has the UN done about these failures?

There have been several attempts at reform of its decision making structure and to strengthen the authority of the UN. The main problem is getting member nations to agree!

In 2005, the UN agreed to widen membership of the Security Council to countries such as Germany, Japan and Brazil. However, the veto holding permanent members: UK, USA, China, Russia and France, still dominate. President Obama has pledged American support for reforming the Security Council and giving India a permanent seat on it.

It set up a new principle in global security – the "responsibility to protect" peoples from genocide when national governments do not take action. A "Peacebuilding Commission" was set up to supervise the reconstruction of countries after wars. This is designed to complement the intervention principle by offering help as well.

Ultimately, the UN is only as strong as its members allow it to be. For example, the new Human Rights Council includes UN members with some of the worst human rights records.

Western governments wanted the new council to be smaller, more effective and with members chosen on the basis of their human-rights records. Instead, the new body has 47 members and is open to all. One of its members is China. Although China became party to the UN Convention Against Torture in 1988, the government has not taken effective measures to diminish the risk of prisoners being tortured or ill-treated. Defendants in China can be, and are, put to death for criminal offences, including non violent property crimes such as theft, embezzlement and forgery.

What is NATO's main role?

NATO was founded in 1949 with the expressed aim of defending Western Europe against a military invasion by the Soviet Union. Its aims can be summed up in the immediate post-war phrase "keep the Russians out, the Americans in and the Germans down."

When West Germany joined NATO in 1955, the Soviet Union formed its own "Warsaw Pact". The 1980s was a period which saw several international flashpoints between the USA, led by Ronald Reagan, and the Soviet Union. The arms race and theory of "mutually assured destruction" provoked a growth of peace movements across Europe. The collapse of the Soviet Union, and with it the Warsaw Pact, meant a strategic re-evaluation of NATO's purpose, nature and tasks.

If Soviet style communism was no longer the enemy, a new danger emerged in the aftermath of 9/11: the global terrorism of al-Qaeda and the Taliban. The 9/11 attacks invoked Article 5 of NATO's Charter, which states that any attack on a member state will be considered an attack against the entire group of members. Russian leader Vladimir Putin called September 11 a "turning point" in Russia's relations with the USA and NATO.

So, NATO today has a new focus?

Very much so. NATO has moved a long way away from its Cold War roots. Indeed, it has expanded its membership eastwards into former Soviet bloc states. In 2008, NATO invited Albania, Romania, Georgia and Ukraine to join. In April 2009, Albania and Romania joined, giving NATO 28 member states. Both Georgia and Ukraine have not, as yet, joined. Both are concerned that NATO membership may harm relations with Russia.

The 2010 Lisbon summit was a re-affirmation of NATO's post-cold war roles. It set up the Emerging Security Challenges Division (ESCD) whose focus is on combatting terrorism, the proliferation of Weapons of Mass Destruction, cyber defence, and energy security.

Defeating the Taliban in Afghanistan is vital for NATO. In 2010 the NATO-led coalition has suffered over 600 deaths, the highest number since the American invasion in 2001 and part of a steadily mounting trend since 2003. The mission has become increasingly

American dominated. But, the UK has played a major part. The UK still believes it is better to "fight the terrorists in Afghanistan than on the streets of London".

How has NATO dealt with recent threats to peace and security?

NATO had a regime building role in Iraq. In August 2004, in response to a request by the Iraqi Interim Government, NATO established a Training Implementation Mission in Iraq. NATO is involved in training, equipping and technical assistance – not combat. The aim of the mission was to help Iraq build the capability of its Government to address the security needs of the Iraqi people.

In August 2003, NATO commenced its first mission ever outside Europe when it assumed control over International Security Assistance Force (ISAF) in Afghanistan. This was confirmation of NATO's new role: that of counter-terrorism.

NATO now emphasises the need for better intelligence, and more unmanned aircraft that can loiter and spy and attack. These are all capabilities aimed at fighting an enemy like al-Qaeda, one with no formal structure, in the information age.

NATO has achieved a degree of success in Afghanistan. Schools have been built. Electricity and clean water have been provided. Roads have been built; an infrastucture has been created. The Taliban have been removed from power and Afghanistan has its own elected Government. Democracy, though, is fragile. Afghanistan is listed by Transparency International as one of the most corrupt Governments in the world.

And it has been at a cost. There have been almost 2,000 NATO casualties in Afghanistan since 2001. The Taliban have proved to be a stubborn enemy. Civilian deaths incurred by NATO during the campaign, a general distrust of the West by the Afghan people and Taliban propaganda have made the war in Afghanistan a long and hard one. Many are now questioning if the war is winnable and if the sacrifices made by so many will be in vain.

Have there not been tensions with Russia?

Yes. NATO's expansion into Eastern Europe is seen by some in Russia as a continuation of a Cold War attempt to "encircle" and isolate Russia. Russia's fears intensified when the Czech Republic, Hungary and Poland became the first former Soviet bloc states to join NATO.

In April 2007, NATO's European allies called for the creation of a ballistic missile defence system (BMD) in Poland to protect Europe from missile attacks. Russia saw this as an attempt to undermine its nuclear capacity and even claimed that such a deployment could lead to a new arms race. But, relations have since thawed. Lisbon brought Russia on board, offering the country the possibility of working with NATO on a new BMD, aimed at protecting Europe from attack from Iran, rather than Russia.

In April 2010 Russian President Dmitry Medvedev signed the nuclear arms reduction treaty START with President Obama in Prague, signalling a much more harmonious relationship. In May 2010, NATO troops participated in Moscow's annual May Day parade for the first time. In August 2010, NATO announced that it was joining with Russia in a new counter-piracy initiative in the Gulf of Aden.

Yet, in December 2010, Wikileaks revealed the existence of "Eagle Guardian", NATO's secret plan for defending several eastern European countries in the event of aggression by Russia. This is the first time since the end of the Cold War that NATO has actively seen Russia as a threat to global security.

What about relations with China?

Interestingly, China as it achieves super power status, has formed its own global security alliance, the Shanghai Co-operation organisation (SCO).

SCO was formed in 1996 and now has six full members: China, Russia, Kazakhstan and Kyrgyzstan, Tajikistan, Uzbekistan. These countries account for 60% of the land mass of Eurasia and its population is a third of the world. With observer states included, the SCO accounts for half of the human race.

While the SCO does not declare itself as hostile to NATO, the fact that it refused entry to the USA underlines the fact that the SCO is an attempt by the eastern powers, with their vast energy reserves, to counter-balance, at the very least, NATO's influence.

Notes